SOME KINDA GOOD

SOME KINDA GOOD

GOOD FOOD AND GOOD COMPANY, THAT'S WHAT IT'S ALL ABOUT!

REBEKAH FAULK LINGENFELSER

Some of the articles in this book originally appeared in the *Statesboro Herald*,
in Rebekah Faulk Lingenfelser's food column,
Some Kinda Good, between May 2013 – April 2019.

Comments and suggestions are welcomed.
For information, email *SKGFoodBlog@gmail.com*.

First Edition

RebekahLingenfelser.com | SomeKindaGood.com

Cover design by Tori Ivey Sprankel
Book design by Wordzworth Limited
Foreword by Bill Fortenberry

Photographers: Rebekah Faulk Lingenfelser, Tori Ivey Sprankel,
Ryan and Tricia Smith, Andrew Sherman, Esther Griffin, Paprika Southern Studios,
Kurt Lingenfelser, Angela Nicole Smith, Laney Golden and Chef Alex Lewis

Printed in the United States of America

ISBN 978-1-7330188-0-7 (print)
ISBN 978-1-7330188-1-4 (epub)

"FIND SOMETHING YOU'RE PASSIONATE ABOUT AND KEEP TREMENDOUSLY INTERESTED IN IT."

—JULIA CHILD—

FOR SMALL TOWN AMERICA AND ALL THOSE WHO HELPED TO SHAPE MY PERSPECTIVE OF FAITH, FAMILY AND FOOD

Contents

Introduction

This book is a timeline of my journey to present day, a window into a world of risks, dreams and possibilities, my heart poured out on its pages. I invite you to read the stories of my life in real-time, to witness a series of events unfolding—the raw moments of defeat and frustration, the surprising discovery of new flavors and foods, the victorious celebration of dreams come true.

I hope you'll find each of the 10 chapters written with soul and enjoyable to read, while learning some tried and true cooking techniques along the way. You can start from the beginning, or from whichever chapter you find most attention-grabbing. Chapter 10 includes a special collection of my most cherished recipes, including others sprinkled throughout the book, so no matter where you are, you can bring *Some Kinda Good* cooking and the flavors of the coastal South into your own kitchen. I've also included a collection of Georgia restaurant reviews from the spots I frequent along the coast, in my hometown of Augusta and my husband's hometown of Savannah. There are a few special stops I've discovered in my travels too, in South Georgia and beyond.

When I reflect on my life over the last few years, the hand of God has never been more evident. My best laid plans are no match for the path He has set before me. In 2015, just two months after my husband and I married, I lost my job due to corporate cutbacks. I was ultimately devastated and couldn't understand why, when I was thriving at seemingly the height of my career, such a setback could happen.

Six months later when no full-time job had yet surfaced, I set my sights on something I'd always wanted to do: culinary school. Without a job, I knew financing this endeavor would be a challenge, so I began researching scholarship options. What I discovered was something far better: I obtained a grant for dislocated workers and was able to pursue culinary school without a penny out-of-pocket. Flash forward to 2017, I was working full-time again as a marketing director in health care. It was the week of Thanksgiving, after 5 p.m., and I was at my desk still working when the phone rang, an area code I didn't recognize. When the caller on the other end of the line said he was from the Food Network, my heart began beating so fast I could hardly contain it. I went on to compete on Food Network Star, a show I had dreamed of doing and worked hard toward—food writing, performing live cooking demos, blogging and cooking, for so many years. Today, I have a great job in a beautiful city, back in a career field I love, the one that's always been my bread and butter: marketing and public relations. The funny thing is, when I interviewed for the job, I was recognized from Food Network, and the story of how I got there played a big role in getting the offer.

You see, had it not been for the corporate cutbacks, I would have never gone to culinary school. Had it not been for culinary school, I wouldn't have been as prepared for Food Network Star, and had it not been for Food Network Star, I may have never gotten to tell my story. I'm so thankful my plans didn't work out. Every step had a purpose; every trial, a silver lining.

I began my blog with one idea in mind, a quote from the late Julia Child who said, "Find something you're passionate about, and keep tremendously interested in it." *Some Kinda Good* was born out of necessity, as a creative outlet to my day job, but also during a time in my life when I needed something to pour myself into, something that was completely mine to shape and mold. It was November of 2011 and my first marriage was coming to an inevitable end. *Some Kinda Good* provided a place where I was free to be me, a place where I could share the recipes that made me happy and the stories that shaped who I am. In the process, I had no idea the opportunities blogging would bring about and the plans the good Lord had for me. When you do what you love, success comes. So many of my dreams have come true because I found something I was passionate about and kept tremendously interested in it.

When I reflect on my accomplishments in culinary entertainment, it all started with *Some Kinda Good*. I hope my story inspires you to be fearless in the pursuit of what sets your soul on fire, and to go confidently in the direction of your dreams. We get one life to live. Always go after the things that make your heart beat.

Much love,

Rebekah

Foreword

I clearly remember our first meal together.

Rebekah's eyes widened the minute the Santa Fe waitress delivered a basket of warm yeast rolls to our table. It's a crying shame the chef who baked them didn't see her reaction. Rebekah tore a roll in half, picked up her knife and smeared the soft butter on the exposed insides.

"Sweet Jesus!" she said, inhaling the still-rising steam. She took a big bite, and all time stopped. I've searched for the right words to describe Rebekah's appreciation for that meal, and none are adequate: amorous, appreciative, satisfied. That's not "satisfactory," mind you. That's slap-your-mama SA-TIS-FIED.

Over the next few years I discovered that it wasn't just lunch rolls that elicited that kind of response. Pasta Primavera? "Bless!" Peanut butter cookies? "Praise the Lord!" Stuffed peppers? "Y'all!" A red-white-and-blue, Fourth of July blueberry and strawberry shortcake? "YAAAASSSS!"

Rebekah Faulk Lingenfelser loves food. Her newspaper column, blog and social media presence are tributes of her devotion to all things tasty.

This book contains a couple of fancy French words, but if your idea of an enjoyable meal is looking down your nose at a plate containing exactly one snail, one arugula leaf, a carrot and a smear of wine sauce, you might want to skip on over to something more pretentious. If it never occurred to you that eating local is not a 21st century concept or that you can grow your own vegetables in a galvanized wash tub, this one might not be for you.

If, however, you come from a family where holidays revolve around ovens and stovetops in a kitchen where it's OK to use canned ingredients, then you should definitely keep reading.

Rebekah and I worked together in health care public relations early in her career. Our shared appreciation for words, the South, food as fellowship, laughter, music and Jesus is the basis of a friendship that I still treasure. This girl's passion for food, her drive and her confidence have taken her places most of us only dream about, and I can't wait to see where this road will lead.

Wherever it leads, I know this:
The journey is going to be *Some Kinda Good*.

Bill Fortenberry

Family Traditions

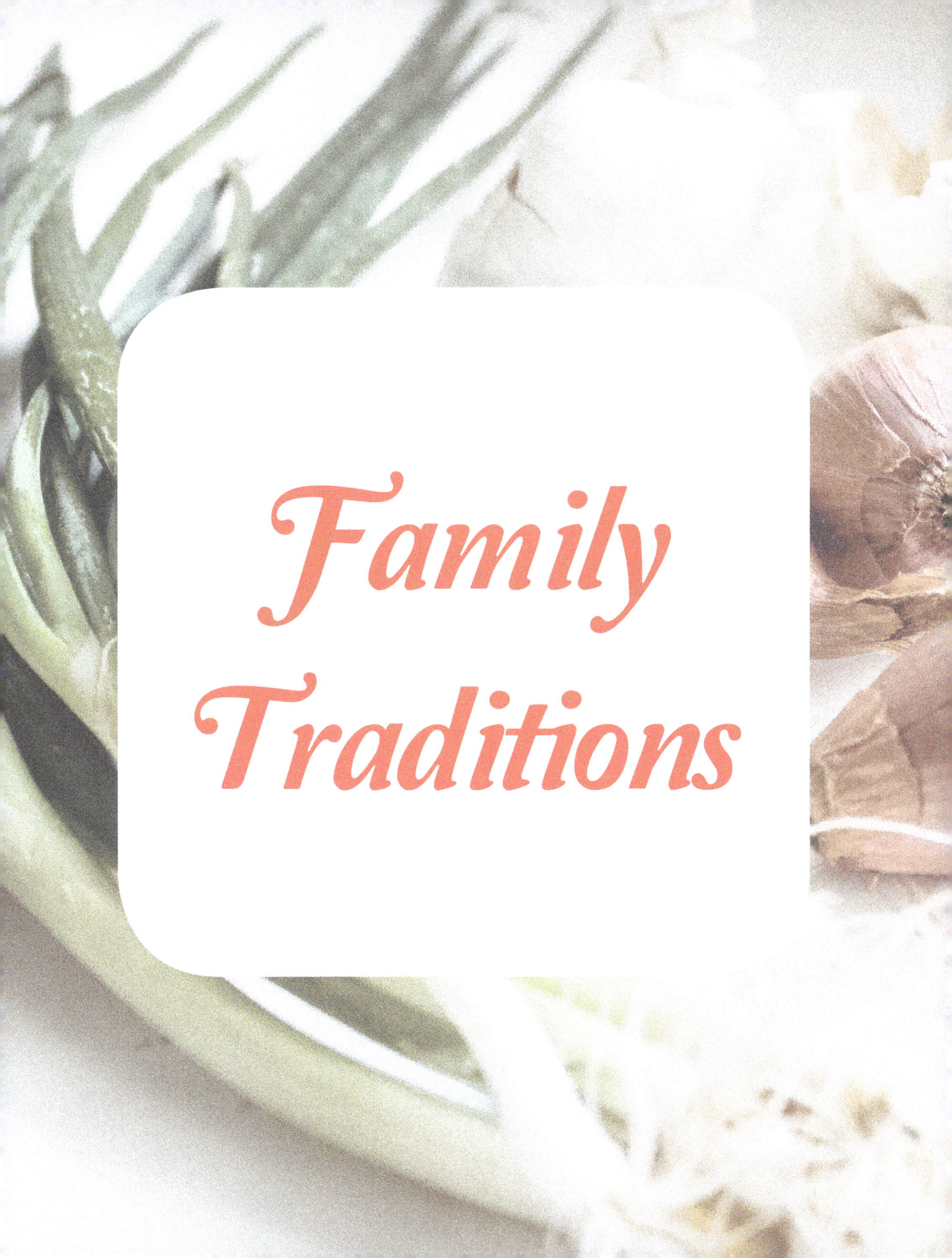

A Rich Tradition at Richland Baptist Church: Dinner on the Grounds

October 8, 2017

On the first Sunday of October at Noon every year, my family shares the time-honored tradition of attending Homecoming and Dinner on the Grounds at Richland Baptist Church, known fondly to the locals as "Old Richland." Since the 1800's, family and friends have gathered among the Middle Georgia pines of Twiggs County to worship and fellowship. With a nip in the air, this year was no exception. The service is reverent, the food is plentiful, and the people are like coming home.

A landmark on the National Register of Historic Places, Richland Baptist Church was built on October 5, 1811 and began with four male and eight female members. Situated down a long gravel road, the large-frame, white wooden church is constructed with a wide front porch and four columns that stretch across the front of the building. Complete with two aisles on the inside and three sections of long wooden church pews, the tall windows, dressed with black shutters, reach nearly to the rooftop. The original heart-pine wooden floors creak with rich history, and the chime of a metal church bell–three times–still signals the beginning of service. True to the original time period, the church has no modern-day amenities; guests still use outhouses for restrooms. There is no sound system, but truth be told, microphones and speakers aren't missed; the acoustics in the expansive room produce some of the most beautiful sounds my ears have ever heard.

During the 206th Anniversary Celebration this year, a gentleman by the name of Russell provided the special music for the service. With only a guitar, he sang a heartfelt solo and then led the congregation in a melody of hymns, inviting others to sing along. Upon the strum of the first cord, without hesitation, every church member lifted their voices in unison. As the harmonies filled the air, I was touched by the powerful sense of place, the belief we all share in faith and truth echoing in the melodies. The familiar songs, "I'll Fly Away," "I Saw the Light" and "Amazing Grace" are written on our hearts, memorized from our youth and, like a freely flowing river, run through our very veins.

Once the service is over, everyone piles out of the church and onto the grounds, forming two lines down either side of a 40-foot cement table filled with every Southern covered dish you could imagine. Heaping baskets of fried chicken, pork tenderloin, barbecue, Brunswick stew, buttermilk biscuits, casseroles, congealed salads and a variety of cakes, pies and cobblers fill our plates in true Baptist fashion. This year, I made sweet potato pie and an old-fashioned heirloom tomato salad with cucumbers and onion. There were no leftovers.

Much like the music that bears witness to my upbringing, the foodways of a land are never more proud than Dinner on the Grounds. The banquet table in all its glory is the Song of the South, the anthem of farmers, the prized recipes of generations gone before us.

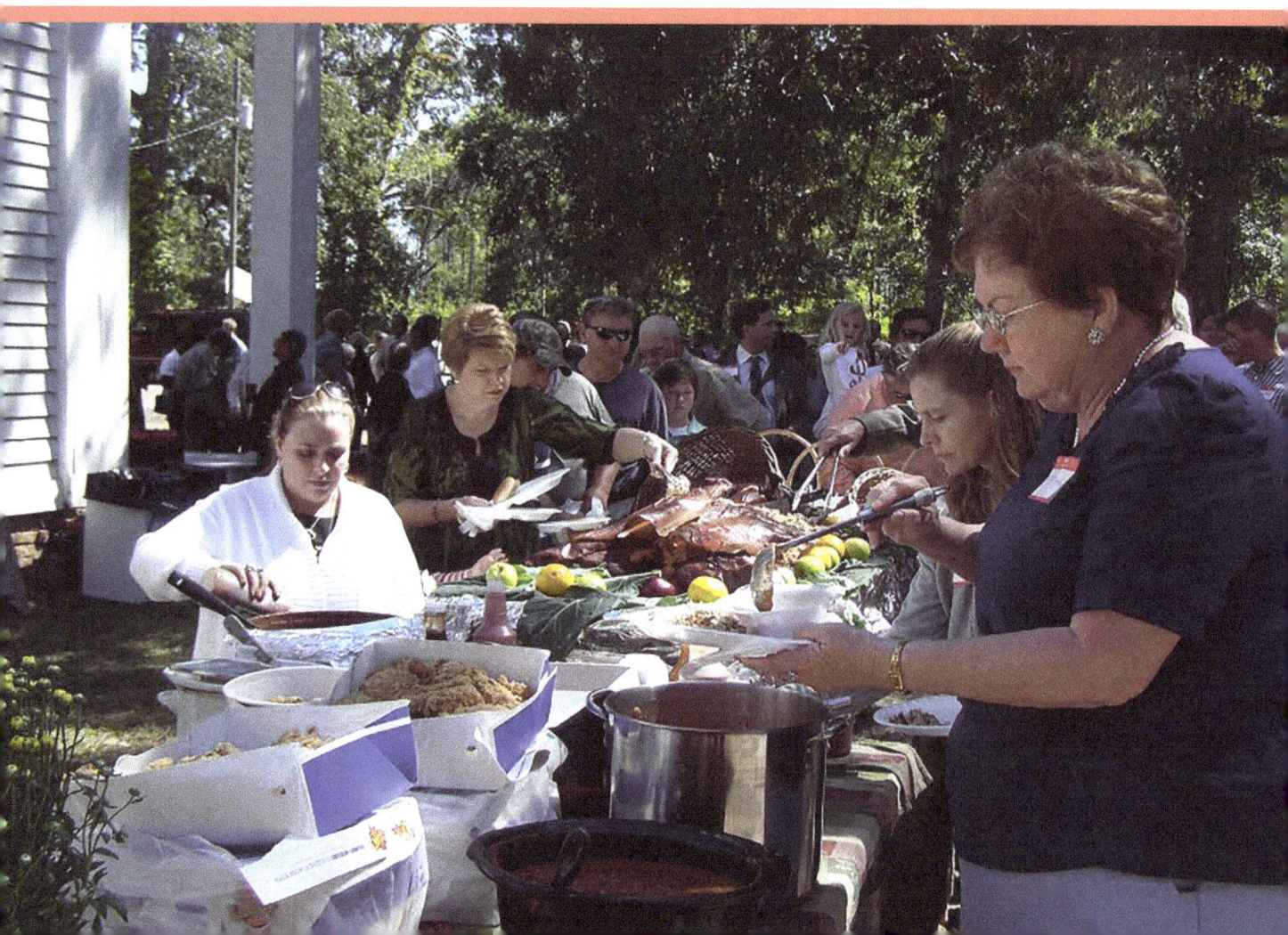

Today, Old Richland is managed by Richland Restoration League, a volunteer committee formed to ensure the upkeep of the building and the grounds. Services are held only three times yearly, for Homecoming and a special fundraising event during Christmastime. Though the locals now meet every Sunday at *New* Richland, a small country church just a few miles away, with such modern amenities as air conditioning and running water, we all look forward to that special fall day when the doors at Old Richland open once more and the church bells call us home.

Thanksgiving Traditions: A Celebration of Family and Food

November 21, 2017

Growing up, Thanksgiving was always an exciting holiday. Both my parents' families are large, and each year we would alternate which side to spend it with – the Faulks in Macon (my dad's family) or the Coopers in Augusta (my mom's family). No matter where we were, two things were always constant: lots of good food and togetherness. Today, Thanksgiving is much the same, only now I have my husband's side of the family from Savannah to throw in the mix. It's safe to say, holiday season around my house means we're on the road a good bit, but that's always been the norm for me.

The host of Thanksgiving, usually one of my aunts and uncles, is responsible for the turkey. All the other relatives bring side dishes and dessert, and there's enough food to feed an army. One year, my Uncle Tommy and Aunt Susan made two turkeys – one was roasted in the oven and the other was deep fried. That was memorable. I recall liking the roasted turkey best for its moist meat and pretty browned skin (to achieve this, use lots of butter).

After so many years of eating together, certain family members have become known for making a signature dish. For my mom, it's her sweet potato casserole with a pecan-streusel topping that's always a hit. My Aunt Susan makes a mean mac and cheese and a wonderful cold grape salad with cream cheese and brown sugar. My Aunt Kathy's biscuits and her coconut cake

don't last at the table long, and Grandma Dot's pound cake shines among all the pumpkin and pecan pies. I come from a long line of good cooks.

As for me, I don't have that one dish that defines me yet. I see Thanksgiving as a blank canvas to create. To be honest, in the beginning of November, I love to flip through the pages of *Southern Living* or *Taste of Home* magazines and discover those recipes that make for a delicious and stand-out presentation. I will often make an ambitious dessert that's on the front cover of the magazine, and I always bring an unpredictable side dish that adds interest to the menu. With all the heavy casseroles there, I like to think outside the box and liven up palates with something fresh. The moment you arrive to the party with your masterpiece in hand, everyone buzzing about, asking what you brought, makes for a fun entrance.

In recent years, I've made a pumpkin cheesecake, cranberry-apple pumpkin Bundt cake, a pumpkin spice cake with chocolate pecan filling and a rustic dried cranberry and Granny Smith apple tart. My must-have side dishes on Thanksgiving include roasted Brussels sprouts with bacon and Parmesan cheese and that good old-fashioned pineapple and Ritz cracker casserole I look forward to eating so much.

It also wouldn't be Thanksgiving without canned cranberry sauce. In many ways, I like to be adventurous but at the same time, I'm a die-hard purest about other things. Canned cranberry sauce is one of those things. I've made it from scratch with fresh cranberries and orange peel, but fresh cranberry sauce just doesn't do it for me. The canned cranberry sauce, little ridges and all, is the only suitable accompaniment topping my turkey.

This year and every day,
my heart is grateful.
Happy Thanksgiving
from my family to yours.

The Cookin'

At the end of a long dirt driveway lined by 23-year-old pine trees in Middle Georgia, sits The Old Home Place, where my family has celebrated "The Cookin'" each Christmas for more than 30 years.

Since the mid-1950s, the Faulks have gathered in Twiggs County during Christmas week to eat, drink and be merry–and to slow roast hog meat in an outdoor, handmade fire pit. "The Cookin'" began as a prerequisite to Christmas Day, when the pork would be the main event at the Faulk Family Christmas Party.

For as long as I can remember, "The Cookin'" has been a part of my holiday experience. I can't imagine a Christmas without it.

Growing up, The Old Home Place was my granddaddy's house, a large white wood framed home with a wraparound porch, where my dad and his four siblings–two brothers and two sisters – were raised. My granddad, Joe W. Faulk, Jr., or as he was nicknamed, Baby Joe, carried on his father's tradition and passed it on to his children, who keep the practice alive still today.

About two days before Christmas each year, my dad and uncles rise before dawn to pick up the hams and pork shoulders, slab side ribs and tenderloins from the local meat packing house and return them to the pit, a 4 x 4 foot construction made of stacked cinder blocks fitted with a large grill grate and covered with a sheet of plywood. The meat starts cooking in the early morning for upwards of eight hours. Smoked sausage is grilled alongside the hams to keep hunger at bay throughout the day.

In the backyard near the pit, an age-old makeshift fire barrel stands tall and serves two purposes: creating oak and hickory wood chips for the pit and putting off heat to tame the chill in the December air. Two 55-gallon metal drum barrels, ends removed, have been welded together, and a hole cut in the bottom just big enough to fit a flat shovel. Each time a log is added to the top, embers float into the air, dancing against the sky.

The day is filled with casual chatter about fishing, memories of relatives gone on and laughter between the five siblings who are all grown now with children of their own. Sounds of good music like, "Jeremiah was a Bullfrog" and Hank Williams' "Family Tradition" set the tone as aunts, uncles, cousins and kinfolk gather around, sit on tailgates and walk about. Pets wander in the yard, and children play games on the property. As the hours pass, neighbors and friends come and go as they please, bringing snacks and desserts to share.

Around 4 p.m. when the meat is hot off the grates, it's time to get down to business. My uncles transfer the pork to a side table

and pull it apart by hand. My granddaddy's special recipe of barbecue sauce is added, and the meat is wrapped up and put away to be eaten on Christmas Day, while other hams are divvied up for individuals to take home.

"The Cookin'" was once just a common part of my family's holiday routine, but as I've gotten older, I've come to appreciate the rich tradition it is today. Food ties us to our traditions. It's the thing that makes us feel good and connected. Even though my Papa passed away when I was just 13, one taste of that fine Georgia barbecue and it's as if he's right there by my side. I can see Baby Joe now scooping those wood chips from the bottom of that barrel and shoveling them into the pit.

When it comes my time to carry on the family tradition, I'll continue it with great honor, together with my brother and our cousins. On this Christmas, I'm so grateful my ancestors began "The Cookin'" so many years ago. It will be an event that creates lasting memories for years to come at The Old Home Place. From my family to yours, Merry Christmas.

From The Heart

Food for the Soul:
A Feast for Uncle George

August 25, 2013

Georgia is the only place I call home. Though I've spent summers in the Pacific Northwest and traveled to Europe on more than one occasion, I am convinced for a number of reasons that the Southern United States is truly God's Country—our culture and our traditions are unlike anywhere else I've been.

Last Sunday, the oldest living member of the Faulk family went home to be with the Lord. He was my Great, Great Uncle George who would've been 97-years-old in November. A WWII veteran and farmer, Uncle George was born in 1917. His funeral, complete with a 21-Gun Salute by the U.S. Marine Corps., was held at a little country church, with less than 10 pews, in the town where he raised his family, farmed the land and lived out his days. It had been some time since I'd been to a memorial service, but there in the fellowship hall as we ate and celebrated his life, I was reminded of the comfort in familiarity. I found myself surrounded by the dishes that shaped my childhood, those dishes that every good Southern cook rushes to their cupboards to fix when there's a death in the family, a newborn baby or a reunion, those tried and true recipes that can only be found in spiral bound cookbooks, produced by the Junior Leagues or church ladies in our communities, or handwritten and passed down through generations.

As we filled our plates, the lineup of traditional classics didn't disappoint—Fried chicken, fresh shelled black-eyed peas, cream corn, broccoli and cheese casserole, pineapple and Ritz cracker casserole, rice with gravy, cornbread and dinner rolls. For dessert, my Dad asked me to "whip us up a 'nana puddin'," but I knew better. That popular dish would be chilling in someone else's refrigerator before I could even get to the store for my ingredients–and duplicating wasn't an option. Sure enough, layered beautifully and elevated in its trifle dish, the highly requested dessert sat front and center on the table, surrounded by pound cake, angel food cake with strawberries and cream, and my blackberry cobbler.

My culture taught me that food is more than a meal–it is the way we show love and compassion, say thank you and offer our deepest condolences and congratulatory blessings. Sometimes when words aren't enough, the food does the talking. New York Times Bestselling Author, the late Pat Conroy said: "In the South you often eat as well after the burial of a family member or friend as you do on Thanksgiving Day or Christmas. It is the custom of the place for friends to bring a dish of delicious food to the home of the deceased—it is one of the binding social covenants that still survive in even the most estranged enclaves of the South." I know my Uncle would've loved the feast. Rest in peace George W. Faulk.

Table Talk and Family Ties

September 24, 2013

We all know the saying, "If these walls could talk," but if my family's kitchen table could speak–boy, could it tell some stories. I'm fortunate enough to have been raised eating around the family table, and every day I'm thankful my parents made it a priority. In homes across the world, the kitchen table, much like the front porch, is an iconic, central hub, especially in the American South.

Formal dining rooms are different.

I'm talking about the table in our eat-in kitchens–the one we cook just steps away from, where we stack our bills at the end of the day, where kids complete their homework, where the family pet begs for that taste of human food.

When I think about the people in my family who've sat around that same oak, oval-shaped table year after year–even the loved ones who are no longer with us–and all the abundant food that's been presented there, along with the memories it holds, the conversations it keeps and the prayers its heard, I consider that togetherness a real blessing. Those moments make a house a home.

Around the kitchen table, we've celebrated birthday after birthday, eaten holiday meals, opened Mother's Day cards and decorated Christmas cookies. It's there every time I visit home. Like an old friend, it's the one constant that's part of the family too, ready to welcome us, inviting us to sit for a spell and stay a while. There, I

eat my mom's homemade chocolate chip muffin with one candle for breakfast each year and introduce new friends to the family. It's the ultimate place boyfriends are bring-home-to-mama-and-daddy tested. We set it with our everyday dishes and fine china. We adorn it with fresh flowers and fruit. There, we hold hands around it and bow our heads to pray.

Without it, home would not be the same.

Sure, I'm one to curl up on the couch with a bowl of cereal now and then in front of my TV, but nothing beats sitting down to a home-cooked meal and a place set just for you, to share good food with the people you know, and who know *you* and where you came from.

So much of my life has taken place at the family table and often, it's the memories associated with that central element that have created the values and traditions I cherish today. I am a firm believer in the popular phrase, "The fondest memories are made gathered around the table."

My Moment with the Queen of Southern Cuisine

August 14, 2014

The evening I met the Queen of Southern Cuisine began in true Savannah style with cold beverages from the bar – Pinot Grigio for me and a Yuengling for my handsome – and live music – a classic Ray Charles cover song, none other than "Georgia On My Mind," performed by two talented guys with their guitars and perfect harmonies. The lights turned down in the Lucas Theatre and the sounds of Georgia on my Mind filled the auditorium. They played two more songs, The Allman Brothers' "Ramblin' Man" and "Chicken Fried" by The Zac Brown Band, perfectly appropriate before Paula Deen took the stage.

And then, there she was. After all the years I'd watched her on TV and imagined her voice as I read her books, there she was not more than 125 feet standing in front of me. She and her husband Michael came out dancing. Her son, Jamie Deen tweeted a photo from backstage of Paula and Michael with a caption which read, "Seeing Mom dance makes me happy." It did my heart good to see them too, resilient and carefree – A stark difference from what the media would have us to believe. He twirled her around on stage as the audience clapped, hooped and hollered. I must admit, I got a little teary eyed, and nearly patted my boyfriend's kneecap off in excitement. Her boys, Jamie and Bobby trickled out some time after that. I was so starstruck, I don't remember them entering the stage. Immediately, it was as if I was seeing an old friend, hanging out with Paula and her family in their living

room. There was no formality, no script to the show. Paula was the exact same in person as she is on television. When she spoke, she began recognizing faces in the audience, pointing out her new daughter-in-law to us all (Congratulations Bobby!), and acknowledging other friends and relatives that had come to see her. She is the personable, warm and sweet spirited woman I have grown to know and love, oozing with Southern hospitality and authentic

drawl. Right away, she told us what we could expect from the show, with a funny interjection from Michael.

Throughout the night, the tugboat captain was like a parakeet, chirping witty things whenever the moment struck: The night was filled with great audience interaction. At one point, Paula called a Look-A-Like up on stage. We played "Deen There, Done That," hosted by "Bobby Chewbanks" dressed in full costume, complete with a wig and an old-fashioned sport coat. Later, Bobby told us a funny story about his Grandma Paul (God rest her soul), who lived to be 91. He said she use to take her medicine with a pull-tab Budweiser Tall Boy.

Paula spoke to a packed house. I don't believe there was an empty seat in the Theatre. During the event, she cooked up three dishes with help from the family: a Georgia Peach Trifle, a Chicken Arugula Salad and Jambalaya. Next to meeting Paula, my favorite part of the show were the short video clips they shared. We got to see how Michael and Paula met and even got an inside look and mini tour of Paula's beautiful home on Wilmington Island. Her rags-to-riches story was shared, including a look back at "The Bag Lady" days. Many audience members had eaten those first lunches.

After the show, I got to meet and talk with Jamie and Michael. Jamie was as nice as he could be. He looked at my boyfriend Kurt who is born and raised in Savannah–and took a double take. "Don't I know you?," Jamie said. Kurt replied, "I'm from Savannah. You may have seen me around." Then Jamie said, "Yeah, I'm pretty sure I've poured you a glass of sweet tea or two." CLASSIC!! You can't make this stuff up.

Michael and Paula met because of Paula's Shih Tzus, Sam and Otis. Me and Paula have even more in common than Southern, coastal cooking, y'all! I bet she'd love my sweet Shih Tzu, Ewok.

The moment finally came when I would have my chance to meet Paula. I received no special treatment; it was every man for himself. About the time I approached the stage, I heard her bodyguard say, "Okay, last one folks. Paula's got places to be." Panic set in. I couldn't be in the same room with Paula and not at least try to get a photo. This opportunity may never present itself again!

Just before she walked off the stage, I managed to jump in and snap three pitiful selfies. I also handed her a copy of "It Ain't All About the Cooking," and she quickly scribbled *Paula* on the inside cover. And just like that, she was gone. So close, but so far away. Will this lady ever know how much she's influenced me in the kitchen? Will she ever know it's my dream to cook with her? So much to say, so little time. I am a better cook because of you, Paula. Thanks for paving the way. Paula, if you read this, know that your fans are so glad you're "getting butter every day." We never doubted you would.

That Awkward Moment When Someone Labels Me a "Food Critic"

March 26, 2015

It happens all too often, and most assuredly slips off the tongues of the most well-meaning people. A common misconception, an innocent remark on the road to Hell paved with good intentions. In the awkward and embarrassing seconds that follow, the damage has already been done; the label already applied. It's that first impression introduction where a good friend is excited to introduce me, to brag a little about my success–and it's almost always in front of someone who has worked incredibly hard in the food industry. It goes something like this:

The person introducing me to {Insert stranger}: "Hey, so-in-so! I want you to meet my friend Rebekah. She's a food critic."

Screeeeeechhhhhhh. First impression fail. No. No. No. Can you say *awkward*?

It's happened upon meeting the restaurant owner on my first visit to a new eatery. It's happened while shopping at my local farmers' market on Saturday morning. It happens commonly at work functions and social events. And I get it. I really do.

People think it's cool and different that I write about food. They enjoy sharing that my blog is one of Urbanspoon's top Georgia food blogs and that I was a contestant on Season 2 of ABC's *The Taste.* Some like to tell about my writings as the *Statesboro Herald* food columnist or that my Grilled Georgia Peach Recipe

wound up on *The Dr. Oz Show.* While I sincerely appreciate the enthusiasm and support, there's absolutely nothing worse than being labeled a "critic" of any kind, much less of something

I dearly love and respect, and more importantly that utterly contradicts the very nature of my personality. Ask any one of my best friends and they would tell you that I would find the bright side of the situation even if my life mirrored The Book of Job (okay, maybe that's a bit extreme, but you get the point).

I created *Some Kinda GOOD*, and I emphasize the *GOOD*, because my mission has always been to bring positive attention to the chefs and restaurant owners out there doing amazing things. Whether it be a mind-blowing dish or a super passionate cook, I love sharing great food discoveries and cool places with others. In the more than three years that *Some Kinda Good* has been in existence, you won't find a negative restaurant review on my blog because honestly, I have much better things to do with my time. Who am I to criticize the creation of someone else's dish, when Lord knows I've butchered too many a meal to count. Furthermore, I can't conceive of a more arrogant attitude than to think I would go out to eat with the intention of judging every morsel of a dining experience. I actually enjoy eating, and don't get my kicks by broadcasting negative opinions about other folks who're just trying to make an honest living. That's simply Some Kinda *Bad*.

If you've seen the fantastic movie "Chef" starring Robert Downey Jr., and Scarlett Johansson, you'll remember the scene where a famous and influential food critic visits a restaurant for the second time after writing a terrible review. The head chef confronts him face-to-face in the public dining area and completely loses it. That scene captures every single reason why I never want to be THAT GUY.

So, if we're ever out in public together and you'd like to introduce me to someone, do me a huge favor and please consider this: "Hey so-in-so!! Meet my friend Rebekah. She's a food *enthusiast*."

It's way more accurate, lacks the negative connotation and doesn't make me want to crawl under the table. Thanks for that.

When My Job Quit Me

January 18, 2016

Life is full of curveballs. One year ago, on this very week, I was packing my bags for Charleston, so excited to begin my new job in a brand-new city. I wrote to update you on my where-abouts; you may remember the post "All Things New in 2015; *Some Kinda Good* Greets the Lowcountry." Today, I find myself packing yet again, this time for a city not-so-brand-new, and with feelings more somber than excited.

The shocking moment came on a Wednesday afternoon, during a weekly routine meeting with my boss. I had been with the company just eight months and two days. Things were fast-paced and extremely busy, but going well. "As you know, HCA is over budget," she'd said. "I'm so sorry, but I've been asked to eliminate one position in our department, and unfortunately, that position is yours." The words hit me head on like a MACK truck. Like a deer in headlights I sat stunned, rendered near speechless, my mind spinning a hundred and one miles per hour. I had come to the meeting prepared to brief her on the multiple projects our team had going, and within mere seconds, none of those projects mattered. A "Reduction in Force," would explain my departure to future employers, and a severance package would lighten the blow. Suddenly and abruptly, the Charleston dream was over before it ever really began, and the world again was wide open. Just as I was climbing the corporate ladder and getting use to the lure of The Holy City, my job had quit *me*, leaving in its place deep disappointment, frustration and a lot of decisions to make. In the words of the late Dr. Martin Luther King Jr., "We must accept finite disappointment, but never lose infinite hope."

With that said, we're moving home to Georgia. This Friday, we'll take Highway 17 to Interstate 95, then to Interstate 16 where the live oaks and palmettos give way to the scrub pines and flat lands of Claxton, Georgia. The Fruitcake Capital of the World will be a temporary landing, a good, quiet place to collect our thoughts and plan our next adventure. There, this country girl can dust off her cowboy boots, which I never once wore during my whole year in Charleston.

Experiencing something so out of my control really has a way of putting things in perspective and helping me to count my blessings. I may be losing my luxury apartment with all its bells and whistles, but the things that matter remain: My husband, Kurt, is my #1 cheerleader and biggest fan. I have the greatest friends and family in the entire world. I have a valuable education, a solid foundation of work experience to build upon and in the words of my parents, "A good head on my shoulders." My job search may take some time, and though I may not know what tomorrow holds, I am confident in who holds tomorrow. The silver lining through this entire experience is time and opportunity. Though 2016 is filled with many questions, I am fueled with hope and excitement for what lies ahead. I've already got a few leads up my sleeve and I can't wait to share them with you!

On this Martin Luther King, Jr. Day, I will remember this quote, "The ultimate measure of a man is not where he stands in moments of comfort and convenience, but where he stands at times of challenge and controversy."

Here's to starting over again, because giving up is never an option.

Keep Calm and Carry on Cooking

March 24, 2016

With only a few days before Easter to go, I know I should be writing about ham and sharing egg-cellent recipes. The truth is, there's something else weighing heavy on my mind that I've been dying to share with you. Since I started my food blog in 2011, a large part of my inspiration has come from this Julia Child quote: "Find something you're passionate about and keep tremendously interested in it." 2016 is the year I take that philosophy to the next level. You can attribute it to 10 years of being in the workforce or the clarity that comes with the decade of turning 30, but no matter how you slice it, experiencing a situation such as When My Job Quit Me, has provided raw perspective.

Tomorrow, with orientation and class registration, the next step toward my goals in culinary entertainment become real. I'm adding **student** to my list of descriptors! I've decided to go to culinary school.

Blazing a new trail at the ripe old age of 32 is scary and all together crazy in some ways. I have moments filled with doubt and if I'm being totally honest have fought this open door with so much hesitation. However, there's something riveting about deciding to go confidently in the direction of your dreams and to live the life you've imagined. I truly believe the Lord has placed these desires in my heart and all arrows are pointing in this direction. Going to culinary school use to mean graduating and becoming a chef, but that is not my goal. Today there are so many avenues one can take. I'm thrilled to combine my unique background of marketing & public relations + food writing expertise with a secondary education in culinary arts. To realize my dreams of becoming a food editor for a leading magazine or hosting my own cooking television program will be greatly enhanced with this expanded knowledge.

"The magic recipe to living out your boldest dreams:
A pinch of delusion, a dash of audacity and a shot of courage."

—KIRSTY SPRAGGON, AUTHOR

One Savannah Evacuee's Account: Watching and Waiting Hurricane Irma

September 10, 2017

During a natural disaster, when one is forced to sort through their belongings to decide what to take and what to leave behind, it provides perspective. Tonight, I sit on my parent's windy patio in Blythe, Georgia, a quaint little community outside of Augusta, where my husband and I, along with our 10-pound Shih Tzu, Ewok, and my in-laws have evacuated from Savannah. It's been a long, unsettling and anxious few days, traveling, waiting and wondering if our homes will be standing when we return and what path Hurricane Irma will decide to take. Watching the weather and the news on TV is grueling, as one of the most unpredictable and historically strong hurricanes makes its way passed Puerto Rico and the Bahamas up through the west coast of Florida.

Georgia Governor Nathan Deal called for a mandatory evacuation of Savannah on Thursday last week.

That's when we began packing our bags, praying for the best and preparing for the worst. We set about bringing inside our front porch furniture and securing anything outside with the potential of blowing away during hurricane and tropical storm-force winds. We filled our bathtub with water in case the power is out when we return home. We secured our city garbage cans and got out of town a day before the primary evacuation began to avoid heavy traffic as much as possible, joining the thousands of other Floridians already on the road.

As I sorted through my closet, I chose to bring my best work clothes, my fall boots and some other clothing items that are newly purchased and well fitting. I opened my jewelry box to gather only the most valuable and sentimental pieces – a Claire's friendship necklace that two of my best friends and I share and gave to each other in the 6th grade. It hung on the rear-view mirror of my Z71 Chevrolet Camaro throughout my high school years; a gold seashell necklace left to me from my late grandmother Betty; a gold palm tree necklace that my husband gave me on the day before we wed and a sterling silver sixpence necklace custom made for me on a trip to London from a dear family member. I tossed in a few other pieces of value, before grabbing up some irreplaceable photographs.

From there, I made my way to pack a few things from the kitchen. Oh, my precious kitchen. How could I possibly pack up all the things I hold dear in the heart of my home? My favorite cookbooks, my treasured appliances, my cake stands and cherished dishes. I quickly realized how selfish and insignificant my dilemma seemed, as I considered what cookbooks were worth saving, when others' homes in the Caribbean Islands had already been leveled by the devastation and catastrophic storm surge of the Category 5 Hurricane.

I found myself getting emotional as we locked up the house. Uncertainty and worry, anxiety and fear, all of these emotions whirled through my mind as I pulled out of the driveway. When would we be cleared to come home? Would we have a home to return to? Would a tree fall through the roof? Would flood waters overtake everything? Would my furniture and all the material possessions I'd worked so hard to attain be there when we got back? What would happen to my place of business? Would it too survive the storm? So many thoughts and questions...so much unpredictability.

The scriptures that are written on my heart combat these very thoughts as I pray for that peace that passes all understanding.

Luke 12:25 says, "Who of you by worrying can add a single hour to your life?" I also think of Philippians 4:6-7 which says, "Do not be anxious about anything, but in every situation, by prayer and petition, with thanksgiving, present your requests to God. And the peace of God which transcends all understanding, will guard your hearts and your minds in Christ Jesus."

As of the latest tracking information, Hurricane Irma has weakened to a Category 2 Hurricane and has shifted west, further away from Savannah, although strong winds and potential tornadoes are still a serious threat. No one can really know the impact this hurricane will have on our city and our Nation until it has passed. What I do know tonight though, I am so grateful for: I have the shelter and safe haven of family, a place to go and the means and resources to get there. I am not unaware that so many evacuees are without these simple comforts.

Join me in praying for a weak and quick end to Hurricane Irma. I believe in a Jesus who can still speak to the wind and calm the storm.

Farewell to the Great Pat Conroy

March 5, 2016

The news of author Pat Conroy's death just yesterday evening (March 4, 2016), has wrecked me. Pancreatic cancer took him from us at the age of 70. To feel such a connection to a man I've never met, never looked in the eye or shook hands with is surreal. As we take in the tragic loss of one of the greatest writers to ever grace this earth, that feeling of closeness and sense of shared place is exactly what so many of Conroy's fans are experiencing. Last night as I read the announcement of his passing, my husband, seeing my shock and devastation said, "But you didn't even know him?" Oh, but I did. I knew him through his books. Those who've never read his books will not understand this heartache. Those who have, mourn with me.

In my writing, I have often talked about Conroy—how could I not after he's had such an influence on my life? A master of the English language, never has there been another wordsmith who has commanded words so powerful and moving to inspire me. Of his notorious books, I've read "The Lords of Discipline," "Beach Music," "South of Broad" and "My Losing Season." He may have written "The Great Santini" about his father, but it is Pat Conroy who is truly great. Like so many others will testify, he has made me a better writer and an avid reader. Over the years, his authenticity, raw emotion and transparency on the pages of each of novel have drawn thousands of people in and impacted lives all over the world. Conroy and I share a love of food, the Lowcountry and writing. I read his books to learn and to study the art of truly great prose, and along the way found myself entertained, overjoyed and distraught with hunger for more as a I turned the final page.

I once checked out of the library and cooked from "The Pat Conroy Cookbook." As I wrote when I first tasted one of his recipes, his crab cakes remain The Best Crab Cakes in the World for me. The subject of food was a sacred one to Conroy. In the first chapter of his cookbook, he explains his appreciation for good food:

"My passion for eating springs from a childhood not deprived of food, but deprived of good food. My mother thought cooking was a kind of slave labor that involved women having too many children. She looked upon food as a sure way to keep her family alive, and it did not occur to her until late in life that one could approach a kitchen with the same intensity as an artist nearing a canvas..."

He goes on to include,

"But even my mother could not grow up in the South without accruing several specialties that she could render with casual mastery. She made corn bread that could not be improved upon. I can still smell her apple and peach pies cooling on the windowsills of our house on Spencer Avenue in New Bern, North Carolina. Her lemon bisque made her famous in whatever neighborhood we settled in during my much-traveled boyhood."

For Christmas just this past season, I was gifted the last autographed copy of the cookbook from a local bookstore in the Lowcountry. With tears streaming down my face at the realization he had taken his last breath, I ran my fingers over Conroy's signature and grasped the book close to my heart. If his collection of recipes and stories were a treasure before, they are surely a masterpiece now.

In a 1986 interview with an NPR news reporter, Conroy talks about finding his home in the South. "I'm a military brat. My father was a Marine Corps fighter pilot from Chicago, Ill. I did not live in Southern towns, I lived on bases. I was a Roman Catholic, which is the strangest thing you can be in the South.... when people refer to me as a Southerner... I liked it because I never had a home. It was the first name that was ever associated with me that put me in a place."

If I could talk to Pat now, I would thank him for choosing to make his home in the South. I would tell him we claim him with great pride. We consider it a privilege that he chose the Southern Seacoast to call home. I smile knowing he died surrounded by friends and family in his beloved Beaufort, South Carolina. Rest in peace, brother. Thank you for leaving us with words that will endure eternally and with poetic prose for the ages. Your contribution to this world lives on in your legacy.

Holidays

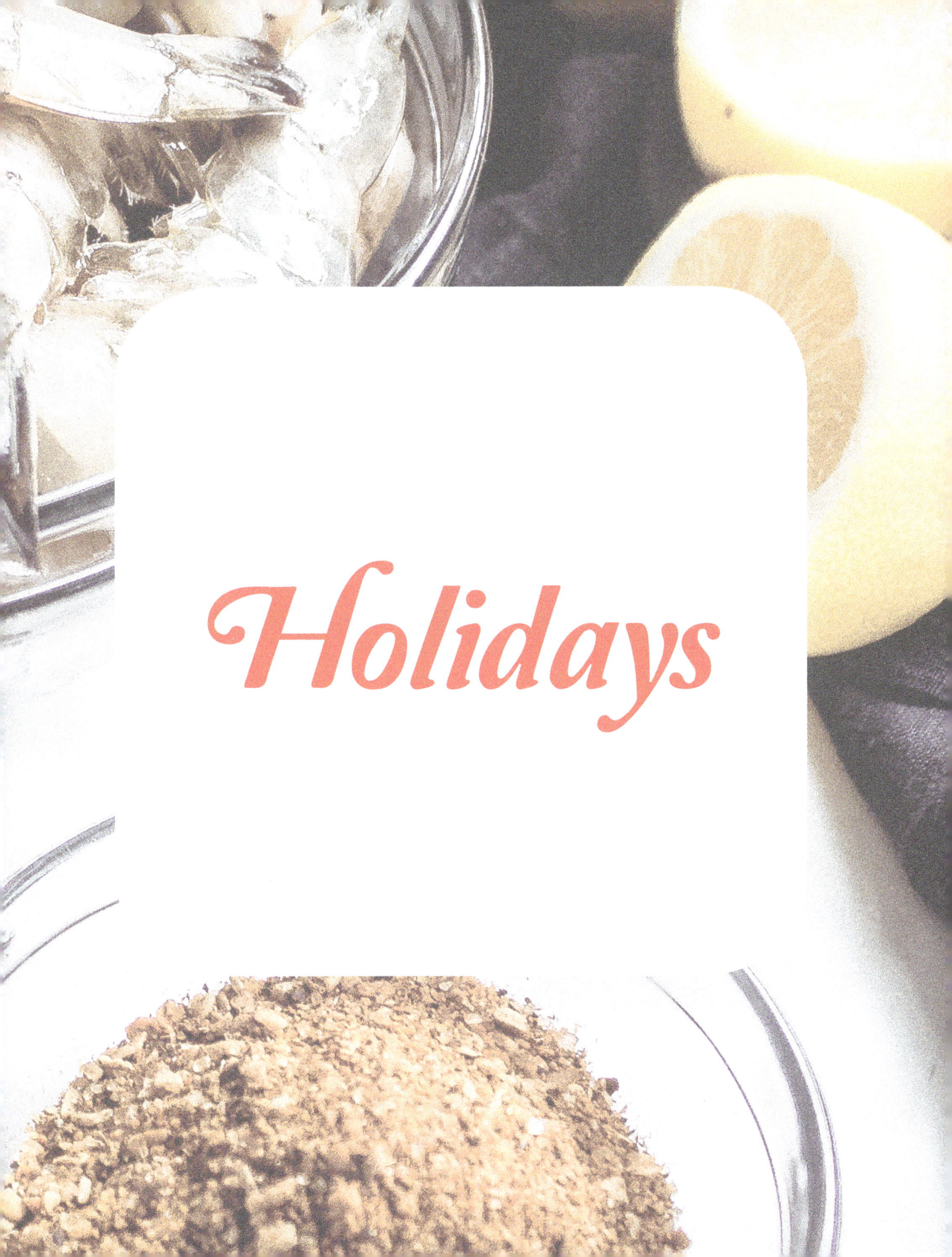

A Valentine's Tribute for My Everlasting Love

February 11, 2018

With Valentine's Day just a few short days away, I wanted to take this opportunity to recognize my #1 taste-tester and good-looking husband, Kurt. Kurt and I met in Statesboro at the Millhouse, and our love story is one for the ages.

It was a pleasant Friday evening, November 2, 2012, and at the time, I worked at Georgia Southern University. A good friend and I had just attended an annual work event where the Swinging Medallions had entertained us until midnight. We had danced the night away and stayed until the very last call, but when the event was over, we weren't quite ready to call it a night. As fate would have it, we ventured over to the hot spot in town to continue the party. I was wearing a blue

cocktail dress and my red high heels. The details of that evening still stand out fresh in my mind, like it was yesterday. I walked into the bar area, and though I didn't know it yet, my husband-to-be sat across the room watching a football game on the big screen. To hear Kurt tell it, as soon as I walked through the doors, he thought, "Business just picked up!" That line always makes me laugh. Soon enough, Kurt and I made eye contact, at which point he seized the opportunity to wink. I blushed, he approached, and in the first few moments of conversation, we got all the priorities out of the way, such as whether he loved Jesus and what he did for a living. I don't believe in wasting time! Though he looked a little scruffy, he had kind eyes and made me laugh. The following Sunday, we went on our first date to the Olive Garden. He had cleaned up nicely. Kurt and I dated for three happy years and decided to tie the knot on our beloved Georgia Coast. We got married in the hot summer sun one August evening on the lawn of St. Simons Island's Lovely Lane Chapel. During our ceremony, I surprised Kurt and sang George Jones' "Walk through this World with Me." It was an unforgettable celebration. We exited the aisle to a foreshadowing tune by Natalie Cole, "This will be an Everlasting Love."

Long before we met, Kurt and I both experienced other relationships and life experiences that made us truly appreciate each other. I've often said marrying him is one of the best decisions I've ever made. Aside from being smart, hard-working and thoughtful, he is well-respected, chivalrous and funny. We share so many of the same interests–food being one of those. We will sit down to a meal and talk about the flavors in a dish or the components of a plate, dissecting every detail with true interest and awe. One of the things I noticed about Kurt right away is his keen palate. In a dish I've cooked or at a restaurant, he will pick up on the smallest amount of cinnamon or a touch of sweetness. He can appreciate a fancy feast such as Lobster Thermidor or Beef Bourguignon, but more often than not, it's the simplest of meals like Manwich sloppy joe sauce over ground beef and tater tots that suit him. I once made him a beautiful beurre blanc, that's a classic French white butter sauce, which I served over pan-seared chicken breast. At first bite, he literally responded in all sincerity with, "Wow, that's better than Parker's secret sauce right there!" Parker's is a popular gas station chain. He keeps me grounded. That's why I love him. So, to my number #1 fan in the kitchen and in life, I quote a line from *Julie and Julia*, my all-time favorite movie. Kurt, "You are the butter to my bread and the breath to my life." Happy Valentine's Day, my handsome.

Have a Sweet St. Patrick's Day

March 17, 2016

It's that infamous time of year in The Hostess City when everyone, no matter who your people are, becomes Irish for a day. Since I met and married a bonafide Savannahian, my life has never been the same. On March 17 each year, come rain or shine, we will don our green and orange, raise our glasses, pack our picnic baskets and join the hundreds of thousands of others in the Spanish moss-covered oak tree city of Savannah, Ga.

As the city's fountains splash with green water and the historic squares and streets fill with the harmonious sounds of bagpipes, it's a time for celebration and rich tradition this Augusta, Ga. native has grown to know and love. Along with the festivities comes a penchant for eating corned beef, shepherd's pie and all things green. Whether you'll be on the Georgia coast with us, or celebrating in spirit from afar, plan to bake my Green Mint Chocolate Chip cookies. They taste great paired with an Irish Coffee. I'll drink to that...Erin Go Bragh! (translation: Ireland forever)

Green Mint Chocolate Chip Cookies

These cookies are easy as pie to bake, y'all. They're basically good old-fashioned chocolate chips, minus the nuts with a few drops of green food coloring. I swap out the traditional semi-sweet chocolate chips for dark chocolate and mint morsels for a surprising depth of flavor.

Preheat oven to 350° F. Combine flour, baking soda and salt in small bowl. Beat butter, granulated sugar, brown sugar and vanilla extract in large mixer bowl until creamy. Add eggs, one at a time, beating well after each addition. Gradually beat in flour mixture. Add green food coloring. Stir in morsels. Drop dough by rounded tablespoon onto ungreased baking sheets. Bake for 11 to 13 minutes or until golden brown. Cool on baking sheets for 2 minutes; remove to wire racks to cool completely.

A Birthday Toast to Savannah's Food Scene

April 26, 2016

Birthdays have always been a big deal in my family, and earlier this month on April 6, it was my turn to celebrate. I took the opportunity for a good time in two parts: First, there was a progressive mid-week lunch with Mom, at the one and only Belford's Savannah Seafood and Steaks in City Market, followed by dessert at Lulu's Chocolate Bar. Second came a Saturday night party with friends: 10 30-somethings descended on downtown Savannah.

As a bona fide food enthusiast and Georgia coast fiend, the city has everything I look for when it comes to the elements of a great party – beautiful surroundings, a lively night scene and captivating energy that permeates the sweet salt air. In this article, I'll tell you about the mouthwatering meals we ate and refreshing cocktails we consumed at some of Savannah's best and most historic hangouts. No matter your age or reason for visiting the coastal city, these stops are sure to whet your appetite.

Long before author Fannie Flagg wrote the famous book "Fried Green Tomatoes at the Whistle Stop Café," which was later turned into a movie, Southern folks were frying up the unripened, garden fresh delicacies—oftentimes out of necessity more than taste. Yet it seems two Georgia girls like my mom and I, just can't get enough of the crispy, tender-on-the-inside goodness.

Rebekah and Jenni Williams

So, it was only natural when lunching at Belford's that we begin our meal with them. Served with a spicy remoulade sauce, both creamy and bright, they were presented on a bed of greens—the light batter covering the tomato completely. Along with our favorite appetizer, we toasted to my year of 33 with bartender recommended cocktails: I had the Blueberry Lemonade sweetened with local Georgia honey and Mom chose the Sweet Georgia Peach Tea made with bourbon and peach schnapps.

For the main course, I ordered Jumbo Lump Crab Cake Sliders with peppery arugula, tomato jam and jalapeño aioli. The bite was soft and sweetly satisfying; the spice and smoke of the greens with the cool texture of jam and plump crab meat made a combination of flavors so complementary, they were tantalizing. Mom had a menu specialty: Shrimp, Greens & Grits. The components of the dish included crisp stone ground grit cakes, Applewood smoked bacon and collard greens, a chardonnay butter sauce, heirloom tomatoes and green onions, topped off with fresh shavings of parmesan cheese. Upon every bite, we reveled in great conversation to the bustling sounds of a happy crowd. What is life? I can't think of too many things more satisfying than sharing an exquisite meal in great company. Belford's also is known for their smoked salmon and certified angus beef steaks.

After a Pedicab ride down to River Street and back, we wrapped up our food exploration with dessert just a few doors down at Lulu's Chocolate Bar. Lulu's Signature Strawberry Suspension Cake has two layers of rum-brushed chocolate cake with a center of mascarpone cheese and strawberries suspended inside. A sleeve of chocolate holds the cake together on the outside. Nothing says party quite like chocolate!

The following Saturday, my friends and I met up at the notorious Vinnie Van Go Go's Pizzeria where we ate customized slices of our favorite toppings, among mine were pepperoni and sundried tomatoes. Next to shakers of grated parmesan cheese and crushed red pepper flakes, cheesy breadsticks and spinach salads crowded the round, metal tables. The satisfying, thin crust pizza left us with full stomachs for a pub crawl through the historic district on a "Boo's Cruise" with Savannah Slow Ride.

We pedaled along the Spanish-moss covered oak tree-lined streets and around the squares singing AC DC's "You Shook Me All Night Long" at the top of our lungs while sipping cold lagers. The tour provided a great way to see a variety of hotspots around the city, such as Boomy's Bar, The Rail Pub and 17 Hundred 90 Inn & Restaurant. Savannah Slow Ride boasts a ton of fun and various cruises to check out and the tour guides offer up entertaining commentary. When the two-hour tour was over, we walked over to McDonough's Savannah Restaurant and Lounge to sing our hearts out during nightly karaoke.

From the fine meal and signature cocktails we enjoyed at Belford's to the casual pizza with friends at Vinnie's and the decadent dessert shared at Lulu's, gourmands will not be disappointed in all The Hostess City has to offer. For locals and visitors alike, Savannah's food scene serves up tons of flavor and fun. I'll drink to that.

Easter Entertaining: Recipes & Recollections

March 30, 2016

Few things bring me greater joy than entertaining family and friends around my kitchen table. Easter Sunday was such an occasion. I hosted dinner for my parents and sweet in-laws, plus my husband's beloved Aunt Polly. From Ina Garten's Coconut Cake to deviled eggs and brown sugar-mustard glazed ham, our celebratory feast was *Some Kinda Good*, and as Southern and traditional as it gets. Though our Smithfield Spiral Ham, with its crispy exterior and sweet, smoky flavor, lived up to all our expectations, the real star and workhorse ingredient of our meal was honey. Used in the glaze for the ham, the homemade dressing for the green bean and cherry tomato salad, the compound butter for the brown and serve rolls and in my Honey Glazed Carrots and Onions, we couldn't have created Easter dinner without it. Hats off to you, sweet stuff.

For me, every aspect of hosting a meal, including menu planning, choosing the festive centerpieces and displaying all my good platters and serving ware is so much fun. On Easter Sunday, I placed green Easter basket "grass" in the center of my black, distressed Pottery Barn table and topped it with pastel eggs of various sizes and flickering votive candles. I even filled a few of the eggs with treats (jelly beans and Reese's Peanut Butter Cups!) for a fun "hunt" at the end of the meal. Adults like to play, too! My bright coral and yellow cotton cloth napkins atop our white bone china made for a colorful table setting and served as the perfect ode to spring.

When I plan a menu, I consider the colors of each dish and how they present on a plate, along with the temperature of the food. Serving too many casseroles or dishes that are all hot or all cold won't provide much variety or any surprises for the palate. Also, considering dishes you can make on the stovetop or in a slow cooker versus in the oven will help maximize space, which is especially important when getting dinner on the table in a timely fashion. Adding unexpected touches, such as a printed menu in a nice picture frame keeps guests on their toes. Any

dishes you can prepare in advance or prep work you can do the night before guests arrive decreases your stress level on the big day. For instance, I peeled and sliced all my carrots, chopped the ends off my fresh green beans and sliced my cherry tomatoes on Easter Eve. Preparing these dishes in advance allowed me to spend more time socializing with family instead of slaving away in the kitchen. When entertaining for any special occasion, changing up where you eat different courses of the meal keeps things fresh and allows the party to flow naturally. After enjoying the main course in the formal dining room, dessert was served with coffee in the casual living area.

Below, I've outlined our dinner menu. Use it as a guide for your next dinner party! Crisp, bright orange carrots, a cold green bean and cherry tomato salad, succulent fall-off-the-bone spiral ham and creamy mac & cheese (in a slow cooker) made the meal one to remember. I've included the mac & cheese recipe – make this and you won't be sorry!

Easter Dinner Menu

- Brown Sugar – Mustard Glazed and Smoked Ham
- Mrs. Debbie's Potatoes Au Gratin
- Mrs. Leslie's Broccoli Casserole
- Aunt Polly's Deviled Eggs
- Honey Glazed Carrots & Onions with Fresh Thyme and Parsley
- Fresh Green Bean & Cherry Tomato Salad
- Slow-Cooker Macaroni & Cheese with Bacon
- Dinner Rolls with Homemade Honey Butter

Dessert

- Coconut Cake
- Mrs. Debbie's Egg-Shaped Rice Crispy Treats

Slow Cooker Mac & Cheese with Bacon

Of all the dishes I prepared, the best decision I made was adding Slow Cooker Mac & Cheese with Bacon to my list of side dishes to serve. Make it in advance by completing the directions in Step 1 up until cook time. Once completely cooled, place the slow cooker in the refrigerator until the next morning when you're ready to cook the dish. Cook four slices of bacon on a baking sheet, then crumble and add on top with fresh parsley to garnish.

Cook macaroni according to package directions; drain. Place in a 5-quart slow cooker; add butter. In a large bowl, mix 3 cups cheese, evaporated milk, condensed soup, 2% milk and eggs. Pour over macaroni mixture; stir to combine. Cook, covered, on low 3-1/2 to 4 hours or until a thermometer reads at least 160°. Sprinkle with remaining cheese. Cook, covered, on low 15-20 minutes longer or until cheese is melted. Sprinkle with paprika. Add bacon and parsley.

Celebrate Cinco De Mayo with the Taco Ring

May 1, 2018

When I was growing up, taco night was super exciting. My mom would bring out this special dish we had with individual compartments for each taco topping. The dish was round, with a circle in the center which was always filled with taco sauce. The other sections were piled high with seasoned ground beef, sharp cheddar cheese, torn iceberg lettuce and chopped tomatoes. She would warm the soft and hard taco shells in the oven, and dinner was served.

With Cinco De Mayo fast approaching this weekend, the Taco Ring is an easy, flavorful and fun way to celebrate! Instead of taco shells, the ring is made up of crescent dough, using a canned tube of crescent rolls. Who doesn't love taco meat wrapped in soft bread? Serve it with sour cream, fresh guacamole and a pitcher of margaritas, and May 5 is made. Cheers!

Some Kinda Good Taco Ring

Serves 8

Ingredients

- 1 medium onion, chopped
- 3 garlic cloves, sliced
- 1 jalapeno, chopped
- 2 lbs of ground beef or venison
- 1 taco seasoning packet
- 1 cup of water
- 1 tube of crescent rolls
- Taco toppings of your choice, such as:
  - Shredded sharp cheddar
  - Chopped tomatoes
  - Shredded lettuce
  - Sour cream
  - Fresh *guacamole*
  - Fresh lime slices

I used ground venison to make my meat filling, but ground beef is awesome in this recipe too.

Heat oven to 375°F. In a skillet, cook beef until no longer pink, along with onion, garlic and jalapeno. Add taco seasonings and water. Simmer three to four minutes or until slightly thickened. Unroll can of dough; separate into eight triangles. On ungreased large cookie sheet, arrange triangles in ring so short sides of triangles form a circle. Dough will overlap. Spoon beef mixture on the half of each triangle closest to center of ring. Sprinkle the top with cheese. **You will most likely have more beef than you need. Be careful not to overfill.** Bring each dough triangle up over filling, tucking dough under bottom layer to secure. Repeat around ring. Some filling will show. Bake 25 minutes or until dough is golden brown and thoroughly baked. Cool five to 10 minutes before cutting into serving slices. Fill the center with toppings.

Thank You Mama

May 4, 2014

As Mother's Day approaches this year, I'd like to tell you a little bit about the lady I call Mama. A strong-willed and feisty God-fearing woman about 5'4 with a small frame and thick, wavy, rich brown hair, she loves a gadget, can't swim and watches the Home Shopping Network and QVC with pure wonderment. To hear my Dad tell it, the UPS man knows her by name. A Tom Hanks movie or good Nicholas Sparks novel trips her trigger. A Saturday might find her spending time with her grandchildren, antiquing, getting a pedicure or going shoe shopping. Independent yet my Dad's other half, career-minded yet the perfect homemaker, if you were to ask any one of my childhood friends what they remember about spending the night with me growing up, it would be her.

When I was in middle school and Mom gave me permission to have friends sleepover, the 12-year-old in us would stay up late talking and doing what little girls do. Without fail we would sleep in late, and if we weren't awake by 10 a.m., Mama was knocking on the bedroom door saying, "Rebekah? Girls? It's time to wake up. What would y'all like for breakfast?" Then she would proceed to list our options presenting them in a waitress-like fashion. "We've got eggs, bacon, pancakes, grits, biscuits, sausage, orange juice, milk; I could fix some waffles or French toast, whatever y'all would like." To this day, my best friends of 20 years still count it among their favorite memories

of us together, reenacting the scene in utter exaggeration. Back then I didn't know it, but not everyone's Mama is June Cleaver incarnate.

As a teenager on a Saturday morning and even now when I visit home, I would wake to the smell of buttermilk pancakes wafting up the stairwell and the sounds of my Mom downstairs in the kitchen, closing cabinet doors and rattling pots and pans. I couldn't wait to wash my face and get to the breakfast table. In the colder months, if I came downstairs barefooted, inevitably at first sight of me, she would say "Where are your bedroom shoes?"

Throughout my childhood, Mama took me to softball practice and attended all my games. A birthday never went by without a big to-do, either at the skating rink or celebrated at home with cake and ice cream. There was never a doubt in my mind that I was special. Come the first day of school, I was always outfitted with every school supply and stitch of clothing I needed. When I walked across the stage for my high school and college graduations, Mama was right there in the audience taking pictures, waving and cheering me on.

With more than 25 years of experience, my Mother has made her living in education, climbing the ranks from elementary school teacher to various leadership and administrative positions. She taught me about professionalism and going after my dreams without ever realizing it.

It is because of her that I love the beach, animals and have my sense of style. Mom introduced me to artists like Toni Braxton and Celine Dion, my first influences outside the country music genre. I inherited that same feisty, go get 'em attitude from her and my love of accessories. She is the reason I'm known among my friends as Martha Stewart.

I have a feeling that throughout my life, no matter if I'm 31 or 80, when I walk in the kitchen barefooted, Mom will always ask about my bedroom shoes. Lord willing, she'll always be right there in the audience, no matter my stage of life.

Mama, I see myself reflected in you. The few examples I've shared today couldn't begin to skim the surface of the childhood you and Dad gave to my brother and me, but as this Mother's Day nears, know that every trip we took, every lunch you packed and every conversation we shared was taken to heart. Today I honor you; I thank you and I love you.

Rebekah's mom, Debbie Faulk

Rebekah's Dad, Joe W. Faulk, III

From the Pond to the Pan – Here's to You Dad

June 16, 2013

I've often been called "a chip off the ol' block." I am my father's daughter, there's no doubt about it. We're built just alike. I have his eyes and his exact feet, only mine are prettier. I get my trademark curly hair from Daddy. We love a classic country song and the Georgia coast. We like good eatin', going fishing and front porch rockin' among the pine trees on our home place. We love pickin' and grinnin' and spending time singing Southern Baptist hymns and 1990's Alan Jackson hits. We're a lot alike, my Daddy and me. On this Father's Day, I honor you, Joe W. Faulk III.

A friend to many and the oldest of five siblings, my Daddy is a well-respected, recently retired welder and electrician whose earned an honest living over the last 30 years in the International Brotherhood of Electrical Workers union. He and my mom just celebrated their 36-year wedding anniversary. I come from an all-American family and that's about as good as it gets.

Some of my fondest memories as a kid were going fishing with Dad. He would bait my hook and let me hold the rod. He showed relentless patience every time I'd cast my line and inevitably get it tangled in a tree or on a log. I'll never forget the thrill of watching that orange and white cork disappear into the water as I reeled in that first fish with all my might. Daddy would holler "You've got a big 'un Bek!" and I would beam with excitement. We'd joke about who could out-fish who, and he always let me win.

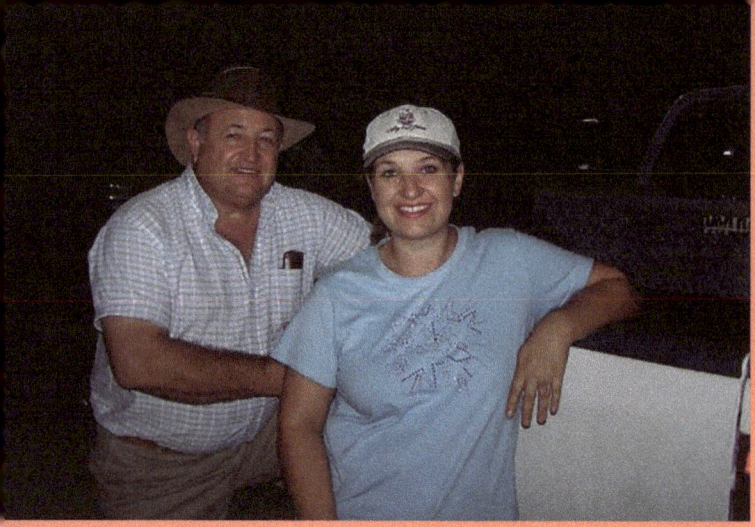

Just recently, Daddy and I took the boat to the river one afternoon and found a quiet cove to anchor down in and fish. The two of us had gotten settled and were happily listening to the birds chirping and enjoying the calmness of the water when suddenly, out of nowhere about three feet from the boat, jumped an otter. The otter did a flip in the air, landed right back in the water and was gone as fast as it came. Left pointing and reenacting the event, Dad and I were both startled in amazement. The otter event remains one of our favorite moments together on the water.

Today, we do most of our fishing on the family pond in Twiggs County where we catch largemouth bass and red brim. When the fish are biting, Daddy will catch him a mess and clean them. Mama does the cooking. For Sunday dinner, she'll roast the fish skin-on, tail and all in butter and simple seasonings, like lemon-pepper and Old Bay. From the pond to pan, the tender white meat is *Some Kinda Good* y'all, but be sure to watch out for those bones.

Throughout the stages of my life, Dad has taught me many things. As a child, he taught me to wash my face and brush my teeth before coming to the breakfast table. As a teenager, he taught me to check the oil in my car and change a tire. Now that I'm grown, there've been times I've wanted to hop the country and leave it all behind, but each time, Dad has been there to say, "Keep your wits about you." My Dad keeps me grounded, sets me straight and instills confidence in me when I need it most. He's as tough as nails, yet compassionate too. He's made sure my brother and I know we've always got a home wherever he is. He's the finest God made and that's all a daughter could ever need.

Happy Pappy Day Daddy, here's to you.

72

A Fourth of July Friendship

July 3, 2016

You can never really know the moment when a forever friend may walk into your life. That fateful day for my best friend of more than 20 years and I, happened in our sixth period physical education class at Hephzibah Middle School, circa 1994. Charity was born on the Fourth of July and ironically, it was Martina McBride's song "Independence Day" that began our lifelong friendship.

Call it destiny or a mere childlike curiosity, but the first words I ever spoke to Charity as she sat near me on the gym floor were, "Can you sing?" There's no guidebook on how to make friends when you're in your adolescent years and I'm not sure what made me think of that foreshadowing question. Looking back on it, it may have been my way of finding common ground. I love to sing, and I knew we would get along well if she said yes. Sure enough, Charity turned out to have a beautiful voice. She replied ever-so-humbly with, "People tell me I can." I don't remember the words that transpired next, but in the following minutes, we must've discussed some songs we knew and which one she should sing to demonstrate her ability. She began singing the first verse, and right then and there, a friendship was born between two sixth graders.

Charity and I went on to sing in middle and high school choir and at church and weddings together, becoming the very best of friends on and off the stage. It was music that united us, and a kindred spirit that would keep us together. We've faced tragedy, celebrated life events, cried over broken hearts and laughed at the silliest of things. We were college roommates and bridesmaids in each other's weddings. During every milestone in my life, Charity has been constant, like fireworks on the Fourth of July.

Since we were 11 years old, I've called her every year on the patriotic holiday from somewhere on a beach. Just as natural as grilling, wearing red, white and blue and Old Glory flying, so is talking to Charity on Independence Day. For Charity's sweet 16, we actually spent her birthday together on Tybee Island and I still have the original filmstrip we took from the fishing pier photo booth. Though we're grown now and miles apart–Charity and her family live near Denver, CO.–come her

Rebekah and Charity Rauls

birthday, Charity knows her phone will ring, and it will be me on the other end. In recent years around mid-afternoon, I dig my cell phone out of my beach bag, step away from my towel and walk towards the surf to give her a call. When she says hello, I launch into singing my signature, over exaggerated Louise Armstrong-like version of "Happy Birthday." As the waves crash at my feet and the summer sun warms my back, we laugh about that extra growl I threw in the song for good measure, or the especially high note I owned while singing it. Then we discuss her plans for the day, which almost always include fireworks, eating cheesecake (she's not a fan of birthday cake) and attending a cookout with friends.

Being born on the same day as a national holiday comes with its pitfalls, but if I had to pick one with which to share my birthday, July 4th would be pretty cool. The whole nation is having a party – let freedom ring! In honor of Charity and our nation's Independence, I'm sharing a recipe for the best cheesecake I've ever eaten. Once you make the buttery crust, a combination of vanilla wafers and pecans, you'll never make a different one. It will change your life! The creamy, cold filling is rich and refreshing. Don't be intimidated by the long list of ingredients. The preparation time is so minimal and the time you put into baking this cheesecake is worth every bite. Make it as festive as you'd like by adding to the top raspberries, strawberries and fresh whipped cream. This dessert will be a showstopper at any cookout, beach gathering or family function. For firecracker flare, try decorating the cake with red, white and blue sparklers. Happy Birthday, Charity, and Happy Fourth of July to you!

Red, White and Blue Cheesecake

Serves 14 – 16

Ingredients
- 40 vanilla wafers, crushed
- 1 cup finely chopped pecans
- ½ cup butter, melted

Filling
- 2 (8 oz) packages cream cheese, softened
- ½ cup butter, softened
- 1 ½ cups sugar
- 2 cups (16 oz) 4% cottage cheese
- 2 cups (16 oz) sour cream
- 6 tbsps cornstarch
- 6 tbsps all-purpose flour
- 4 ½ tsps lemon juice
- 1 tsp vanilla extract
- 4 eggs, lightly beaten

Blueberry Glaze
- 3 ½ cups fresh blueberries, divided
- 1 cup sugar
- 2 tbsps cornstarch
- Fresh blueberries, strawberries, raspberries for garnish
- Fresh whipped cream, optional

Fresh Whipped Cream
- 2 tbsps sugar
- 1 cup heavy whipping cream
- 1 tsp pure vanilla extract

This festive cheesecake makes a firecracker presentation. With its vanilla wafer and pecan crust combined with its rich, creamy filling, don't count on having any leftovers. Baking this cake is well worth the effort.

In a large bowl, combine the wafer crumbs, pecans and butter. Press onto the bottom and 2 in. up the sides of a greased 10 in. springform pan. Place on a baking sheet. Bake at 375° for 8 minutes. Cool on a wire rack. Reduce heat to 325°. In a large bowl, beat the cream cheese, butter and sugar until smooth. Process cottage cheese in a blender until smooth; beat into a cream cheese mixture. Beat in the sour cream, cornstarch, flour, lemon juice and vanilla. Add eggs; beat on low-speed just until combined. Pour over crust. Return pan to baking sheet. Bake at 325° for 70-80 minutes or until center is almost set. Cool on a wire rack for 10 minutes. Carefully run a knife around edge of pan to loosen; cool 1 hour longer. Refrigerate overnight.

For glaze, puree 2 ½ cups blueberries in a food processor; press through a fine mesh sieve, reserving 1 cup juice. Discard pulp and seeds. In a small saucepan, combine sugar, cornstarch and reserved blueberry juice until smooth. Bring to a boil; cook and stir for 2 minutes or until thickened. Refrigerate until completely cooled. Remove sides of pan. Spread glaze over cheesecake. Sprinkle with remaining blueberries; garnish with raspberries, strawberries and fresh whipped cream if desired. To create a star-spangled border, fill a piping bag fitted with a small star tip, with fresh whipped cream. Pipe a border around the cake, until ends meet. To make fresh whipped cream, whip heavy cream, sugar and vanilla in a cold mixing bowl fitted with the whisk attachment, until soft peaks form. Refrigerate leftovers.

A Spirit of Thanksgiving

November 20, 2016

People arrive at thankfulness in a myriad of different ways. We're not naturally born with a heart of gratitude or a spirit of thanksgiving; it's our life experiences and influences that teach us to understand the true meaning of being thankful. For example, just as living in a small Southern town can make you appreciate big city civilization, living in a big city sure has its way of helping you appreciate the charm of a small town. While Thanksgiving Day is a time for feasting, it's also a time for reflection—on the year that's ending, the future ahead and the things that matter most.

If I'm being honest, 2016 has challenged my attitude of thankfulness with great opposition. Time after time this year, my husband and I have faced what seems like a never-ending stream of bad luck. Circumstances completely out of our control have brought about undue stress and grief. Through it all, I've cried out of frustration and struggled with the Good Book's instruction to rejoice in my suffering.

And through it all, I can look and see all the ways I am truly blessed.

Earlier this year, when the not-so-inexpensive fuel pump in my Suburban decided it was finished functioning, my husband had the skills to handle it. When I needed a job that would coincide with my culinary school schedule, the Lord provided one less than a mile from our home. When I was in the hospital recently

for an emergency gallbladder removal surgery, my husband, parents and in-laws never left my side. And when my father-in-law passed away tragically on the day Hurricane Matthew hit the East Coast, our family clung to the only thing we could—strength in the Lord and each other.

When I consider what Thanksgiving means to me, I do well to remember the times I've been humbled, needed help or been down and out — out of patience, money, time and energy. It's during these times my ultimate blessings take center stage: my loving husband, caring family, genuine friendships, a steady paycheck, a good vehicle and my health.

Enduring trials provides perspective and clarity, just as traveling broadens the mind.

During college, I took full advantage of the opportunities I was given to travel the world and experience other countries. I spent the summer of my junior year in one of the poorest countries in Europe, Moldova, located between Romania and the Ukraine. I will never flush a modern-day toilet without remembering the "WC's" (water closets). They were deplorable rooms with small holes in the floor, separated by thin panels on either side. When I ride in my automobile with air conditioning and heat, I won't soon forget the horse and buggies that are still primary forms of transportation there today. And when I attend church for Sunday service complete with big screens, full bands and pyrotechnics, I know full well that the Holy Spirit is no less present in the little shed with a makeshift podium, six wooden benches and a dirt floor in the Moldovan Village across the pond.

The longer I live, the more I realize one can't comprehend the true measure of gratitude unless they've gone without, of food unless they've been hungry, of warmth unless they've been cold. Being thankful isn't posting a cute meme on Facebook or a saying a quick prayer before a meal. It's taking a step back from one's circumstances, choosing to see the good in every situation and understanding that somewhere in the world, someone is less fortunate. Even when our circumstances seem daunting, our experience could always, always be worse.

So, this year, when my plate is piled high with turkey and dressing, canned cranberry sauce, macaroni and cheese, green bean casserole and pumpkin pie with Cool Whip, I'll give thanks–Thanks for every perspective I've gained and every trial that has made me who I am today.

The Heart of Christmas is Priceless

December 21, 2014

When I was about eight years old, I took great pride in decorating my bedroom for Christmas. We lived in a 2-story home in the quaint community of Blythe, Georgia–population 708–and my room was upstairs to the right and down the hallway. It had two windows that looked out onto the street, a small closet, a little white ceiling fan and pink carpet. I had a radio and cassette player that sat on my window seat. The seat was crafted by my late Great Uncle J.E. who was a cabinet maker. In early December, I would clean my room from top to bottom to the tune of the 1987 Reba McEntire audio cassette tape "Merry Christmas to You." Reba was my idol and I wanted to be just like her. I knew every word of the 10-song album, and it was our time together.

As I sat Indian-style on the floor with my scissors, construction paper and Scotch tape, I would sing "Away in a Manger" and "Happy Birthday Jesus" at the top of my lungs in true Reba fashion. I would spell out the letters M-E-R-R-Y C-H-R-I-S-T-M-A-S, then cut the letters out and hang them from the slanted walls. I had one of those miniature pre-lit Christmas trees too, and I thought it was something else. I sequestered myself in my bedroom until I had decked the halls of every square inch of my little space. Once I was satisfied with my handiwork, I would invite my mom, dad and brother into my room to see what I had created. Though my little Winter Wonderland may not have won any awards with *Better Homes and Gardens,* it was something I was proud of and it was good. When I look back on those times or hear a song from the tape, I'm instantly connected to my childhood imagination, to the spirit of Christmas, the hope and wonder of the season. Today that same cassette tape goes for $2.50 on *eBay*, but for me, it will always be priceless.

The holidays have a way of making us nostalgic; nostalgic for those loved ones that we've lost or for friends and family who may be deployed far away. My boyfriend, Kurt, and I visited TMT Farms Christmas Lights Display (a wonderful family activity located on Old River Rd. in Statesboro) earlier this week. On his way to pick me up, Kurt stopped by the grocery store to purchase some canned goods to donate, as there is no admission fee but a Food Drop-Off for families in need. I imagined he would pick up five or six cans, but to my surprise he showed up with three brown paper sacks filled to the brim with sweet potatoes, green beans, black-eyed peas and cream corn. As we drove through the farm admiring the lights, he remembered his beloved Grandmother, who sat in the same seat every Sunday at Blessed Sacrament Catholic Church. He couldn't help but recall how she would buy fresh turkeys during Christmas and donate them to orphanages and to the priests in her hometown of Savannah, Georgia. For him, giving those cans honored her memory, and he was thankful to have the ability to help.

We started a new series at our church recently called "God Gave." A message from our pastor this month reminded us of the hope in Christ and how he came to save us and love us unconditionally. The true meaning of Christmas is about the things money can't buy, counting the blessings we've been given and sharing that love with others.

This season, finding those moments of solitude and reflection have been my saving grace in the midst of my 7-foot Christmas tree toppling over in my living room, trying to mail cards on time, fretting over my shopping list and when I'll have time to bake. As you countdown to Christmas while wrapping those last minute presents, finalizing your holiday menu, sitting in traffic or standing in long lines, I hope you'll take a moment to pause and remember, to give and love others.

In the words of "Tiny Tim Cratchit," a fictional character from Charles Dickens' novel *A Christmas Carol,* "God bless us, every one."

Christmas Ornaments Have a Story to Tell

December 16, 2018

Decorating the Christmas tree has always been introspective for me. Aside from the standard ball ornaments, I have a special bag of sentimental ornaments I delicately wrap and unwrap each year, carefully peeling back the tissue paper to reveal the precious memories. Filled with stories of trips gone by and milestone occasions, the ornaments on my Christmas tree tell the stories of my life.

Growing up, my mom set the example early on. I can never remember our Christmas tree without the red stocking-shaped ornament I hand-fashioned in kindergarten with construction paper, yarn and cotton balls, my name written in glue and dusted with glitter. That ornament is well over 20 years old now, but looks like it was made just yesterday. A clay ornament in the shape of a little boy with hand-painted overhauls and a yellow t-shirt hangs on a branch each year not far from that stocking, made by my older brother when he was in the first grade.

Decorating the tree holds a special place in my heart. I relish the moments when I hang those ornaments on the tree year-after-year, remembering the good feelings associated with each token of friendship or family tie. Each year, a few new ornaments appear with the others, continuing the story of a life well lived.

I took my first trip to New York City this summer, while filming for Food Network Star. I planned my trip with a few extra days on either end, to see the city with my good friend, Jay. From the Empire State Building to the double-decker bus tours, we did it all. One morning, Jay brought me a bonafide New York City bagel to begin my day, complete with a thick slab of cream cheese. Before I left The Big Apple, Jay sent me home with a souvenir: A Christmas ornament in the shape of a bagel with sesame seeds to commemorate our time together in the big city. I couldn't wait to hang it on the tree this year, laughing all the way.

Every summer when school would let out, my family spent the first week of May in Myrtle Beach, South Carolina. I will never forget the excitement of that road trip, my cousin, Justin and I wide-eyed with our Walkmans in the backseat of my mom's minivan, counting down the hours until we could ride the rides at the Pavilion, jump in the pool and swim in the ocean. Without fail each season on our way to the beach, we would stop at the Cracker Barrel in Columbia. Later on in life, I got a job in the Cracker Barrel Gift Shop and couldn't resist purchasing an ornament of the Cracker Barrel itself. Resplendent with Christmas wreaths on each column, rocking chairs on the front porch and a snow-capped roof, I looked at it once, and there I was, an elementary school kid again on my way to the beach, but not before a bellyful of hash brown casserole and pancakes made on a cast iron griddle.

A wedding photo of my husband, Kurt and I, just announced as man and wife while surrounded by friends and family in a whirl-wind of bubbles is framed in a Hallmark ornament inscribed with "Our First Christmas - 2015." I smile each time I see it remembering the start of our lives together. A large sand dollar with a hand-painted deer hangs on the tree, marking the day Kurt shot his first buck. Two other hand-painted sand dollars fill the tree - one with an illustration of Charleston's Rainbow Row, and another of a carefree sailboat on St. Simons Island. A bright red crab basket ornament filled with blue crabs hangs next to them–something to remember our lazy summer weekends crabbing on the Georgia coast.

After a special visit to Dollywood this month in Pigeon Forge, Tennessee, I brought home a new ornament to adorn my tree: A Coat of Many Colors. Based on the inspiring true story of living legend Dolly Parton's remarkable upbringing, the back of the box included an excerpt from the popular song:

My coat of many colors
That my mama made for me
Made only from rags,
But I wore it so proudly.
Although we had no money,
I was rich as I could be
In my coat of many colors
My mama made for me.

What a powerful reminder that what makes us rich isn't monetary material things, but love! If ever there is a time to remember this, it's Christmastime. May you celebrate the love of Christ and family and create memories that will last a lifetime this holiday season. Merry Christmas, from my family to yours.

Travel

New Flavors with Nashville Friends: A Food Adventure at The 404 Kitchen

March 31, 2014

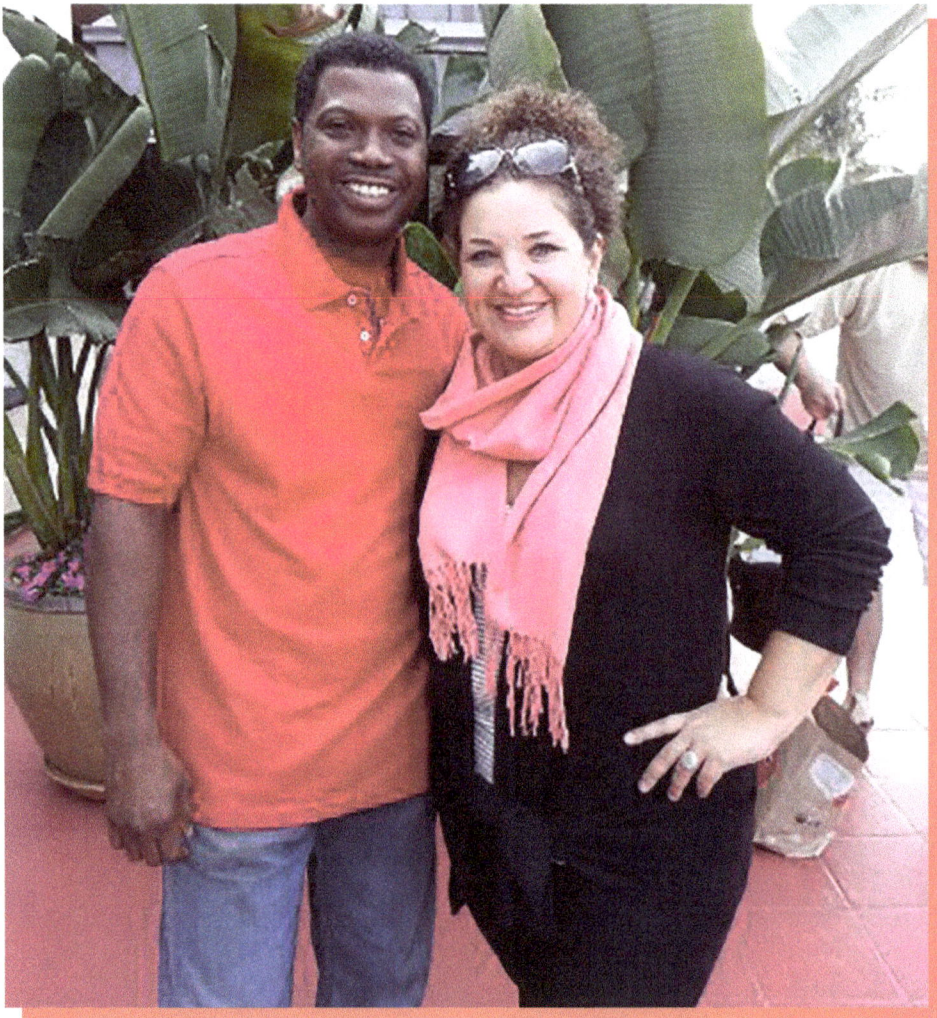

Carlos Davis and Rebekah

The older I become, the more I realize that so much of life is about our experiences. When I auditioned for ABC's cooking competition reality show "The Taste" last year, I couldn't have predicted the friendships that would result and never would have imagined I'd be hanging out in the Music City with the co-owner of an award-winning food truck eating chicken liver pate and drinking cocktails with smoked bacon. I'm talking about my friend, Carlos Davis of Riffs Fine Street Food. You may have seen him on the Cooking Channel's Eat Street or featured in the Nashville Scene. He's the coolest Caribbean I know, with a local, inside perspective on good eats. On a chilly Saturday night in early spring, Carlos and I reunited for the first time since we'd both hopped on a plane Southbound from Burbank, California in September 2013. Carlos showed me around a Nashville neighborhood known as the Gulch, and introduced me to The 404 Kitchen, led by Chef Matt Bolus.

As noted on The 404 Kitchen's website, the restaurant is "Housed in a former shipping container...and offers a modern take on classic European cuisine with an emphasis on local, seasonal fare, including herbs grown on the rooftop garden." A semi-finalist in the Best New Restaurant category of the 2014 James Beard Awards, The 404 Kitchen features indoor and outdoor seating to accommodate 56 guests for dinner, Tuesday through Saturday.

We decided to forgo the entrees all together and jump right in with starters and cocktails. We took our seats at the bar where Carlos quickly pointed out The Nearest Green, a libation featuring Jack Daniel's Single Barrel, Laird's Rare Apple Brandy, Benton's Smoky Mountain bacon and citrus infused Tennessee honey. It had every flavor going for it–fruity, smoky and sweet. Who wouldn't love a cocktail including bacon? I was all in, and it didn't disappoint. When I had finished sipping the cocktail, I shamelessly ate the bits of bacon in the bottom of my glass with a spoon to which Carlos commented, "You would be weird if you didn't!"

The next order of business came in the form of Crudo, an appetizer of Cobia, blood orange, fennel, bee pollen (that's right, bee pollen), pistachio and vidal ice vinegar. Now, I grew up in Blythe, Ga. and Twiggs County farm country. My folks and I didn't eat quite like this. I had no idea what the majority of these ingredients were, but I tasted them with gladness and what a refreshing combination! I learned that Cobia is a type of fish. I loved the crunch of the pistachios and fennel. The vinegar and citrus flavors gave every bite a noteworthy kick. As for the bee pollen, I was at a total loss.

Starter number 2 was delivered on a butcher block: Kennedy Farms Chicken Liver Pate, served with whole grain mustard, pickled radish and the Lowcountry's popular benne wafers. A pate is a mixture of cooked ground meat and fat minced into a spreadable paste. Nothing about that sounds appealing to me, and by the looks of it, you'd think it came directly from a Spam can. Tasting chicken liver pate was another first for me, and the truth is, I really liked it. Reminiscent of humus in texture, its flavor was rich and herbaceous. When the dish came out, I looked directly at Carlos and said, "Alright chef. Teach me how to eat this." He took a healthy portion of the pate and spread it on the wafer, then topped it with a bit of the spicy ground mustard. I asked, "What about the radish?" to which he informed me was a palate cleanser. Makes sense! This home cook surely enjoys having chef friends.

Next up came my pick for the evening, and my favorite of all: 14 Month Aged Benton's Country Ham served with buttermilk biscuits, Tennessee whiskey jelly and red-eye gravy. In the moment the plate came, Carlos tweeted, "#CountryHamAndBiscuits @ The404Kitchen. @SKGFoodBlog just squealed." It was true. I had church with this appetizer. The biscuits were perfection, the country ham was salty and sliced to the perfect thinness, and the jam? I can't. I could have turned the red-eye gravy ramekin up and drank it, but civility got the best of me.

With each new dish, the bartender switched out our silverware and brought new small plates. Lastly, we tried the Burrata featuring celeriac, grapefruit, black truffle, pine nuts, leeks and calabrian peppers. Burrata is a fresh Italian cheese made from mozzarella and cream. Smooth like butter, I'd never known a cheese could be elevated to such heights. Other starters on the menu that night featured Lamb Sugo, Winter Squash Soup and a 3-Cheese Plate. Entrees included Rabbit, Cioppino, Swordfish, Pork Ragu and other mind-boggling dishes. Dining in a place like The 404 Kitchen reminds me of just how much I have to learn about the world of gastronomy.

We wound the evening down with dessert. The grand finale was brioche bread with bittersweet chocolate, and a banana nut loaf alongside cold ice cream. With a daily changing menu, this is a place I could return again and again.

With clean plates and full hearts, we left The 404 Kitchen satisfied, anticipating the next great food adventure. From the service to the atmosphere, topped only by the food, The 404 Kitchen was *Some Kinda Good*, and the perfect spot to catch up with my culinary pal. After all, good food and good company is what it's all about.

My Cruise Vacation of Gastronomic Proportions

October 14, 2014

During the first week of October, I forsook my fall traditions – The Luke Bryan Farm Tour, the Georgia National Fair, Homecoming at Old Richland Baptist Church and the Georgia Southern University Homecoming football game – to sail the open seas on the Carnival Liberty. During my seven-day cruise vacation to the Western Caribbean, I didn't write, cook, work or blog, but...I ate, and what a gastronomic experience it was. This was my second cruise, the first one I'd ever taken with Carnival Cruise lines, and while the food experience varied depending on location in the ship, dinner was the meal I anticipated most, brunch made my heart sing and late night dessert from room service was worth every calorie.

We made four stops during the week: 1) Cozumel, Mexico, 2) Belize, 3) Mahogany Bay/Roatan Island in Honduras and 4) Costa Maya, Mexico. In Cozumel, we lounged in hammocks under the palm trees and were serenaded by three natives and their guitars while eating the best guacamole ever in an entertaining little restaurant called Three Amigos.

In Belize, we sipped rum from a fresh coconut and took a 2-hour tour of the city and countryside. Our ferry-boat also broke down in the Atlantic-Caribbean Coast and we had to return to Belize and catch another ferry back to the ship. In Honduras, we swam in the ocean in the pouring rain, and I got my dad a souvenir–a rosewood guitar pick.

In Costa Maya, I tried a native beer called Sol (tasted similar to a Corona) and I bought my mom a hand-carved wind chime. Now, let's get down to the food. Dinner time for us was 8:15 p.m. each evening. Throughout the week, I enjoyed most the lobster and grilled shrimp. My other favorites were Lobster Bisque, Shrimp Cocktail, Alligator Fritters and fresh fish. I ate a lot of seafood–after all we were on the ocean.

Brunch was served only on days at sea in one of the most elegant dining rooms with big windows. On our first day of travel, we ordered spicy bloody marys and indulged in the French croissants with whipped butter. One night, just for fun, we ordered cheesecake and chocolate cake from room service.

If you ever take a cruise with Carnival, I highly recommend spending your money on what will be one of the most exquisite

and mind-blowing dining experiences you'll ever have: "The Chef's Table." A private dinner with a seating of only 13, you'll get a tour of the kitchen and one-on-one time with the Chef de Cuisine of the entire ship, along with unlimited wine.

The attention to detail, from the correct spelling of my name on both the menu and my place card to the presentation of the plates was absolutely stunning. Chef Singh is one amazingly talented and detail-oriented chef. Every week, he and his team cook thousands of dishes for multiple nationalities representing countless cultures. I have so much respect for the man! I was introduced to so many new concepts and flavors. Air pillows and passion caviar anyone? I left completely inspired, really full and a *little* tipsy. Thanks Carnival Cruise Line, for a vacation to remember.

Some Kinda Good
Goes Shrimpin' on the Lady Jane

September 4, 2015

I grew up in a rural neighborhood on the outskirts of Augusta, Ga. To get to any beach was at least a three-hour ride, but somehow, my soul has always been at home on the water. One of the highlights of my summer was at long last, getting to go Shrimpin' on the Lady Jane with my handsome new husband, and what an excursion it was! I've read so many novels about shrimpin' (check out Mary Alice Monroe's Last Light Over Carolina), and have long dreamt of climbing aboard a real shrimp boat and casting my net. On a rainy August day, thanks to Credle's Adventures, that dream became a reality.

For just $40 a ticket, we got to spend the afternoon cruising the St. Simons Sound, taking in the picturesque views of the Georgia coast and relishing in the wonderment of undersea life. If I hadn't gone to school to study marketing and public relations, I would seriously have considered becoming a marine biologist. The creatures that swim below the ocean absolutely fascinate me! Don't be fooled by the name of the outing—we caught way more than shrimp! Jeffery, the naturalist and guide on our boat, quickly told us that "Shrimp are actually one of the most boring things we catch." Our cast net reeled in everything from two varieties of shark, angel fish, squid, butterfly rays and the most bizarre little creature, called a hog choker.

We cast our 20-foot net twice during the 2-hour event. It stayed down for 16-20 minutes each time. Among the things I learned? How to de-head and devein a wild Georgia shrimp fresh from the Atlantic, that a marine estuary is a mix of fresh and salt water to make brackish water, and all about the oyster beds along the coastline.

Now that I live on the South Carolina coast, I'll be doing a lot more of this! The beautiful green grass along the border of the water is called Spartina and surprisingly enough, this plant gives the water its color. It's the base of the ecosystem's food chain and uses salt water to survive.

I'd recommend this outing to anyone! Y'all know how much I love my Georgia coast, and a good shrimp. One of my favorite ways to cook these babies is to pile them high on a bed of Southern, buttery grits. Thanks to Captain Larry and his crew for a really memorable, fun and great day on the water. We can't wait to go Shrimpin' again!

A Road Trip to Remember

August 15, 2016

As a final ode to summer's end and in celebration of our one-year wedding anniversary, my husband and I took a road trip to visit family on the Mississippi Gulf Coast, a little slice of Southern coastal heaven. Before last week, I had never been to The Magnolia State. I've been missing out! We absolutely loved cruising along the 62-mile stretch of scenic coastline, eating fried shrimp po' boys and dining at the oceanfront restaurants in Biloxi. One sunny day, we even rented a jet ski and boated across the calm waters of Pass Christian Beach. Resort casinos and marinas full of picturesque shrimp boats line the streets, and the few mansions that survived Hurricane Katrina still stand tall facing the shoreline. We shopped in storybook towns like Bay St. Louis, a small community with boutiques and homespun bakeries, where many of the colorful island-style homes feature large screened-in porches.

Anytime I visit a new place, I enjoy trying foods that are home to the region. While we did visit our fair share of chain restaurants like Jimmy Buffett's Margaritaville and Hard Rock Café, one evening, we ate dinner out at Shaggy's. It's a local beachfront restaurant with a large deck that sits right on the sand. A small fishing pole replica sits at each table, and as a way to alert the wait staff, guests simply raise the bobber on their pole. Those memorable and unique touches made the dining experience even more fun. I ordered blackened shrimp tacos and coconut rice, and after one bite, I just had to know how the rice was made. As it turns out, the secret is Pina Colada drink mix! The rice had a sweet flavor and coconut shavings gave it great texture. I plan to recreate the side dish at home and make it my own by adding chopped mango and walnuts.

My husband's grandparents, Fred and Dot, have lived in Long Beach, Mississippi for more than 30 years. Not more than an hour from New Orleans, Louisiana, the food in Long Beach is heavily influenced by its neighboring state. Beignets are not hard to find and po' boys aren't the only sandwiches giving tourists a run for their money. During our visit, Fred and Dot introduced us to the famous Italian sandwich known as the muffuletta, which was invented by a Sicilian Immigrant in 1906 at a New Orleans restaurant named Central Grocery. Both a sandwich and a type of bread, muffuletta is a round Sicilian sesame bread; a somewhat flattened loaf with a sturdy texture, around 10 inches across. Very light, the outside is crispy and the inside is soft. Aside from the sesame seeds, the bread has no additional seasonings baked into it. For lunch, the four of us stopped at a small dive in Ocean Springs, Mississippi and split a muffuletta. The popular sandwich is packed with salami, ham and provolone cheese, and then covered with olive salad. Ours was served warm and cut into fourths. A filling and satisfying meal, the muffuletta is not for the faint of appetite!

Traveling and experiencing new things is one of life's great pleasures. Long after summer is gone, the flavors of South Mississippi will remain in my mind. So long summer, and so long Mississippi.

Vacationing in a Winter Wonderland

December 17, 2017

Nothing brings out the little kid in me like a blanket of freshly fallen snow. Add to that delicious food and quality time with my favorite person, and life is grand. My husband Kurt and I took a mini-Christmas vacation in early December to experience Candlelight Christmas Evenings at Biltmore in Asheville, North Carolina, where we awoke to 10-inches of pure white, fluffy, undisturbed snow. Then, we headed North for Sevierville, Tennessee, where I have a good friend who's a performer at Dollywood. It was a vacation to remember–and the food and wine couldn't have been any better.

For years, I have wanted to visit the Biltmore mansion at Christmastime. I've driven past the billboards many times and never stopped, but this year, it was my mission to get there. Wow, was it something to see. Now, I am officially obsessed with the Vanderbilt family. Dazzled in the most exquisite holiday decorations, each room of the mansion had its own massive Christmas tree that reached high to the ceiling. The harmonious sounds of a perfectly blended children's choir greeted us as we entered the home and a live harpist played softly as tourists walked the expansive hallways. The estate grounds were immaculate and from the shopping to the dining, we loved it all. Our first stop on the grounds was the winery, of course. We each sampled our choice of seven different red and white wines. My favorite was Cardinal's Crest, a medium-bodied soft and easy-to-drink wine with dried

herb aromas, rich blackberry flavors and smooth tannins. The marketing concept is effective: we purchased four bottles to bring home! Just before our self-guided tour through the Vanderbilt home, we enjoyed the most satisfying of meals at a restaurant on the grounds called Village Social. I ordered Frogmore Stew, or as many of you may know it, a Lowcountry Boil. This wasn't your run-of-the-mill sausage, potato and shrimp song though. Resting in the most flavorful, light broth I have ever tasted, and served with two grilled slices of crusty French bread for dipping, the dish included shrimp, clams, lobster, corn, andouille sausage and a mixture of small purple and white tender potatoes. Much to my surprise, when I asked the knowledgeable waitress how the chef prepared the dish, she informed me the restaurant granted recipe requests. I am literally watching my email inbox for the moment this recipe arrives. We finished the meal by sharing a festive dessert: a slice of maple gingerbread cake complete with a gingerbread cookie garnish and hot coffee.

The next morning, we made our way to the Tennessee mountains where we experienced a truly "Tender Tennessee Christmas," at Dolly Parton's Dollywood. We were entertained with a wonderful musical titled "Christmas in the Smokies" which had us all in tears by the end. We then rode a coal-fired train around the park to the tune of Dolly Parton singing Winter Wonderland, oohing and ahhing at the snow-covered, naked tree limbs and Great Smoky Mountains in the distance. In the cold, crisp mountain air as we took in our surroundings, it was a special moment of reflection and peace.

If you've never been to Dollywood, one of the famous park foods is the cinnamon bread. It's a soft, cinnamon-sugar laden twisted bread with doughy texture. You can't visit the park without at least a sample. Even in the snowfall, people stood in line outside for it. We warmed up with hot chocolate and enjoyed this treat, telling ourselves we had walked enough that day to not count the calories.

At the conclusion of our trip, I gathered up my souvenirs, quickly realizing, with the exception of a few Christmas presents, all the things I'd bought were food and beverage-related: Kettle corn, Rocky Road Fudge, Oatmeal Cookie Moonshine (and yes, it's just like eating a cookie!), coconut cream coffee and Biltmore wine. I really am a lover of the finer things in life.

I read somewhere this week that there's scientific proof that a few inches of freshly fallen snow absorb sound. The world definitely seems a little quieter, more calm and still when covered in a seemingly magical blanket of snow. It's as if nature's acoustics are aligned with the hectic holiday season to make us all slow down and simply say "let it snow, let it snow, let it snow." Wherever you spend this Christmas season, I pray it's filled with less noise and distraction, and more moments of peace and reflection. From my family to yours, Merry Christmas.

Kurt and Rebekah Lingenfelser

2017 in Review: My Top 5 Restaurant Experiences

December 31, 2017

On this final day of 2017, I've decided to take a look back at my best dining experiences of the year and share them with you. My job affords me the opportunity to travel, and this year, I got to visit some really fun destinations, and eat some truly inspired food. My work took me to a few places I'd never been before, including Vegas, Ohio and Upstate New York. I also returned to a few familiar states, and at each location, I ate somewhere notable. Whether an appetizer, main course or dessert, each of these dishes were bursting with flavor and made an impressive presentation.

When I visit a restaurant for the first time, I almost always seek out the signature menu item or ask the wait staff about the Chef's best dish. My reasons for this are twofold: 1) For the thrill of eating it and 2) because I learn from it. I enjoy experiencing the flavor combinations and seeing how the Chef plates each component. Creativity and art come together! Today, I'll share my Top Five Restaurant Experiences from 2017, featuring the most memorable menu item of the evening. Maybe these dishes will inspire you to experiment in the kitchen or book your next flight.

1   Flying Fish Café, Orlando, Florida: "Under the Sea"

If you've ever been to Walt Disney World, you may be familiar with the Boardwalk area near Epcot. While there over the summer, I dined at the Flying Fish Cafe. This restaurant appealed to me on so many levels. From the moment you walk in, you feel as though you have stepped inside the sea. With immaculate ambiance and a sustainable seafood and contemporary American menu, I experienced a visually stunning and delectable meal. The grand finale was the restaurant's signature dessert titled, "Under the Sea," featuring: Valrhona Manjari Chocolate (that's a dark chocolate brand which originates from Madagascar with notes of red and dried fruits), Chocolate Coral Sponge, Pistachio Sand, Dehydrated Milk Foam and Tasting of Three Sea Salts. Contemporary cuisine at its finest. What a way to end dinner!

2   Wildflowers at Turning Stone, Verona, NY: Goat Cheese Panna Cotta

While in Verona, New York in June, I ate at my first Forbes Travel Guide 4-Star Rated Restaurant. Wildflowers is tucked inside The Lodge at Turning Stone Resort and Casino. A 65-seat, intimate dining space, my colleague and I sat side-by-side at a booth which faced a large picture window overlooking a fountain and beautifully landscaped grounds. As we awaited the main course, the Chef sent us bites from the kitchen to tantalize your taste buds. On a single spoon, the most beautiful presentation of goat cheese panna cotta with a layer of red currant jam arrived, topped with none other than an edible wildflower. Warm cream and goat cheese are blended together with gelatin and flavored with red currant jam for a savory bite. That single bite set the tone for an unforgettable meal of Dover Sole a la Meuniere classically prepared with brown butter, lemon, capers and parsley. The fish was perfectly cooked, light and beautifully presented. To cook something "a la Meuniere" simply means to first dredge it in flour. Everything sounds better in French.

3   Alligator Soul, Savannah, Georgia: Drunken Mussels

While we're on this notion of fine dining, I couldn't possibly forget to mention a local spot. Alligator Soul in Savannah is a must-visit dining destination. My sweet husband has taken me on a few special dates here, and this year, we celebrated our second wedding anniversary in the underground, romantic space. The menu changes seasonally, ensuring the freshest ingredients with a focus on local, regional and dayboat fare. Among the menu selections is a special section for the Wild & Adventurous. You can order exotic meats such as elk, antelope, kangaroo, ostrich, game birds and red deer. We thoroughly enjoyed the Drunken Mussels in beer broth, presented with sweet peppadew peppers and smoked Tasso ham.

4   Kayne Prime, Nashville, Tennessee: Popcorn Buttered Lobster

You read that right...lobster popcorn! Have you ever heard of such? I love it when a Chef combines a humble ingredient like popcorn with a fancy one like lobster. The name of the dish alone was enough to make me order it. Kayne Prime is an exquisite steakhouse located in The Gulch neighborhood of Nashville. If you're ever in Music City, please eat here. The salty, crunchy popcorn was presented over succulent lobster meat, all drizzled with butter. It was mouthwatering on every level.

5   Village Social, Asheville, North Carolina: Frogmore Stew

In the Travel chapter, you may have read my story about our winter wonderland vacation. I mentioned my favorite dish from the trip, which I experienced at Village Social, a restaurant on the Biltmore Estate. I ordered Frogmore Stew, or as many of you may know it, a Lowcountry Boil. This wasn't your run-of-the-mill sausage, potato and shrimp song though. Resting in the most flavorful, light broth I have ever tasted and served with two grilled slices of crusty French bread for dipping, the dish included shrimp, clams, lobster, corn, andouille sausage and a mixture of small purple and white tender potatoes. I enjoyed the dish so much, I requested the recipe. The Sous Chef himself sent it to me just last week, and it's too good to keep to myself.

In the words of English writer Virginia Woolf, "One cannot think well, love well, sleep well, if one has not dined well." May you dine well in 2018 and Happy New Year to you and yours!

Frogmore Stew

Recipe Courtesy of Village Social Sous Chef Ronnie Collins, Biltmore

Serves 4

Ingredients

For The Frogmore Broth:

- 1 smoked onion, diced
- 1 bunch leeks, sliced and washed
- 1 large carrot, diced
- 1 large rib of celery, diced
- 2 corn cobs, halved
- 8 garlic cloves, whole
- 4 tbsps extra virgin olive oil
- 2 tbsps tomato paste
- 4 bay leaves
- 1 bunch thyme
- 1 bunch tarragon
- 1 cup white wine, such as Sauvignon Blanc
- 1-quart shellfish stock
- 2 andouille sausages, diced
- Hot sauce to taste, such as Tabasco
- Lemon juice to taste
- Salt and pepper to taste

To Assemble The Stew:

- ½ gallon Frogmore broth
- 8 oz corn
- 8 oz sliced andouille sausage
- 8 oz little neck clams
- 8 oz lobster tail
- 8 oz white wine
- 1 tbsp shallot, minced
- 1 tbsp garlic, minced

In a large stockpot or Dutch oven, over medium-high heat, sweat the first six ingredients (all vegetables) in olive oil. Add tomato paste and cook 1 minute. Add wine to deglaze the pan, scrapping up any bits from the bottom with a wooden spoon. Reduce liquid to nearly dry. Add seafood stock, sausage, bay leaves, thyme and tarragon and stir to combine. Add hot sauce and lemon juice, and simmer for 15 minutes. Strain and season to taste.

Simmer all ingredients in enough broth to cover, cook until clams are open and lobster tail is cooked through, serve.

My First Time Visiting New York City

July 29, 2018

In mid-July, I experienced a lot of firsts. I traveled to New York City for the very first time in my 35 years of life. What a different world! There was so much to see and do, and most importantly to eat. I was amazed by the bumper-to-bumper traffic, the millions of people and constant sounds of sirens and honking horns. I was so fortunate to have a native New Yorker to show me around the city, to guide taxi drivers to my next destination and to introduce me to all the things. The culture, the languages, the pizza, the bagels, my first arancini, oh my! I have so much to tell you about.

I visited the 86th floor observatory deck of the Empire State Building. After all the times I've watched "Sleepless in Seattle," I fully expected Tom Hanks and Meg Ryan to walk around the corner at any minute. From the top, I saw the Hudson River and the empty space where the Twin Towers once stood, security helicopters buzzing over 24/7. The skyscrapers, planes and trains were never ending. I rode a double-decker bus and sat on top while sightseeing Central Park and the Upper West Side of New York. The bus cruised Eighth Avenue while riders listened through earbuds to New York-themed music. I was living my best life to the tune of Billy Joel's "New York State of Mind" and Alicia Keys' "Concrete Jungle." I sang and danced in my seat while onlookers questioned my sanity.

I ate soft tri-color rainbow cookies and flaky elephant ears in Little Italy, and nearly died when someone recognized me from Food Network Star and asked me to pose for a photo. I saw dragon fruit in Chinatown and wondered how many storefronts were being disguised by grocery stores and t-shirt shops. I bought a coffee mug from Chelsea Market and stood on a platform in Times Square to have my picture made. Of all the years I've watched Dick Clark and Ryan Seacrest countdown the New Year, it was amazing to stand where the ball drops. Sensory overload to the extreme.

Every day, the food was a real discovery. I celebrated National Hot Dog Day at a restaurant pop-up, with a Chicken Sake

The Season 14 Cast of Food Network Star:
From left: Rebekah, Chris Valdes, Samone Lett, Jason Goldstein, Amy Pottinger, Christian Petroni, Palak Patel, Jessica Tom, Katie Dixon, Harrison Bader and Manny Washington. Front row: Adam Gertler.

Sausage Dog topped with pineapple and jalapeno relish. At an authentic Italian wood-fired pizzeria, I ate the most delectable New York style margherita pizza, pizza with black truffle and robiolona, and these little fried rice balls with pungent lemon flavor, known as arancini. One morning for breakfast, my friend met me with a fresh-made New York style sesame-seed bagel with a thick slab of cream cheese wrapped in parchment paper and I could only eat half. At Alex Guarnaschelli's restaurant, I had a tender New York strip steak with tarragon butter. At one of Bobby Flay's restaurants, I ate roasted octopus with bacon, sour orange and shishito pepper, baked manchego cheese with white anchovy and charred beef with blue cheese, red wine and brown butter. My palate was one happy camper.

The legend Julia Child said it best, "People who love to eat are always the best people." During my time in New York, I was with my 11 new friends from Food Network Star. I wouldn't trade the friendships I made through this experience for anything in the world. Thank you all for supporting me on this crazy journey! They call New York City the City of Dreams, and while it was an amazing place to visit, to explore and eat, I was grateful to trade in the sounds of honking horns for crickets and tree frogs, the taxis for tractors, the concrete jungle for the Georgia pines. "Just an old sweet song, keeps Georgia on my mind."

Food Festival Volunteering

St. Simons Island Food & Wine Festival
Volunteer Experience Leads to Opportunity of a Lifetime

September 24, 2012

It's not every day you meet a living legend. As a volunteer for the Inaugural St. Simons Food & Spirits Festival at Gascoigne Bluff, I got to spend time with the mother of all Southern cooks, Nathalie Dupree, hang out with culinary producers, food writers and some of the finest chefs in the state. I have great aspirations of joining the food world, so this event was truly an opportunity of a lifetime. The event was the first of its kind to benefit the local Hospice of the Golden Isles, featuring four incredible Georgia culinary talents, regional farmers, local artists and over 25 area restaurants. The weather couldn't have been more perfect and the location? Out of this world. When I heard about the festival, it was a no brainer that I participate. Amazing food and live music on the Georgia coast? It's not rocket science!

I was assigned to the Culinary Creations Cooking Stage where the cooking demonstrations took place to help serve and prep food, greet festival guests and clean up and reset the stage after each demonstration. Practically heaven. It was my responsibility to do whatever Crystal, our cooking stage captain told me to do, and I considered it an honor. I did everything from golf cart chauffeuring and fetching pitchers of water for flower vases to picking up lunch for the volunteers. At one point, I was even sent to someone's personal beach house to get several "real" forks. My day started around 8:30 a.m. and ended with the sun setting over the calm water beneath the Spanish-moss covered oak trees.

Hands down, the coolest part of the entire event was my chance meeting with Nathalie Dupree. My most important responsibility of the day was making a run to the grocery store for an extra bag of White Lily Self-Rising Flour for Nathalie. It was of pristine importance that the brand be White Lily. So, there I was driving my tent captain's Volvo around St. Simons Island with a commercial-sized sheet pan of freshly baked biscuits on the backseat, a pound of butter and pint of heavy cream. When I got to the only convenient grocery store on the island, every bag of White Lily Flour was gone. Every other brand was there, but none of them would do. I ventured over to Harris Teeter across the island and luckily found my flour. I made it back to the festival and as I'm carrying the biscuits to the golf cart, who pops out of the SUV parked right next to my ride but Nathalie herself. She said, "Hey, where are you going?" And lo and behold, she wanted a ride. I walked over and hugged her neck and told her that my mom and grandma had been cooking from her cookbooks and watching her on TV for years. She responded with, "How wonderful" and greeted me like family.

If you know anything about Nathalie, she's got a firecracker personality. Later that day, I had an opportunity to take a photo with her. Most folks would say "cheese" when they pose for a photo, but not her. As we were smiling for the camera, Nathalie said the word "sex" just for the pure fun of it. She is something else!

The coolest souvenir I took home wasn't food or drink. It was my autographed apron by the culinary stars I met that day: Nathalie Dupree, Libbie Summers, Ted Dennard and Ford Fry. I intend to frame it with pictures from the event and hang it in my kitchen.

Savannah Food & Wine Festival
Volunteer Perks Result in Lamb and Good People

November 17, 2013

One of my favorite things about volunteering at food and wine events are the people I get to meet. As a volunteer in The Local Palate Celebrity Chef Kitchen at the inaugural Savannah Food & Wine Festival this weekend, I helped greet guests, set up and break down the stage in between talents, collected trash and even got to be a sous chef for Food Network Star finalist, Linkie Marais. I got to interact with festival guests from neighboring coastal towns like Hilton Head S.C., culinary students at Savannah Technical College and Virginia College, and walked away from the event with a 4-pound leg of lamb, a package of mushrooms and one big red onion because I was in the right place at the right time.

Linkie was a finalist on Season Eight of Next Food Network Star. It was awesome to meet someone I had watched on TV last season. She was extremely personable and very friendly. I helped Linkie and her manager clean and chop mushrooms for her cooking demonstration. Plus, they gave me $40 worth of lamb that would have otherwise been discarded. What an awesome, unexpected volunteer perk!

Mrs. Martha Nesbit is a long-time food writer in Southeast Georgia. I got to work with her in the Celebrity Chef tent, and later purchased an autographed copy of her cookbook, *Savannah Celebrations*. I have no doubt that it will become a favorite resource, and I can't wait to dive in to her recipes.

I ran into local Brooklet farmer, Del Ferguson of Hunter Cattle Company at the event. It's always good to see a familiar face when you're out and about. Way to represent Statesboro in The Hostess City Del!

Other presentations included Executive Chef Shaun Doty from Atlanta's Bantam & Biddy, Savannah Technical College, Virginia College and Food Network's Anthony Lamas from Extreme Chef. My favorite presentation of the day was Chef Jean Yves Vendeville from Savannah Technical College's Culinary Arts program. He and his team operated like a well-oiled machine and in his 40-minute cooking demonstration, cranked out three different dishes for the audience to try. He was funny, engaging, educational and entertaining. When his presentation was complete, I told him I wanted to be his student one day.

For Savannah's first ever food and wine festival, the turnout was impressive. Nearly every event was sold out. The Southern, culinary shindig was definitely a team effort and took the hard work of many. I am confident that it will only get better with time. I was honored to be a part of the experience and fortunate to have made such great connections while volunteering. Thanks to everyone who made it happen.

Farmer Del Ferguson of Hunter Cattle Company and Rebekah

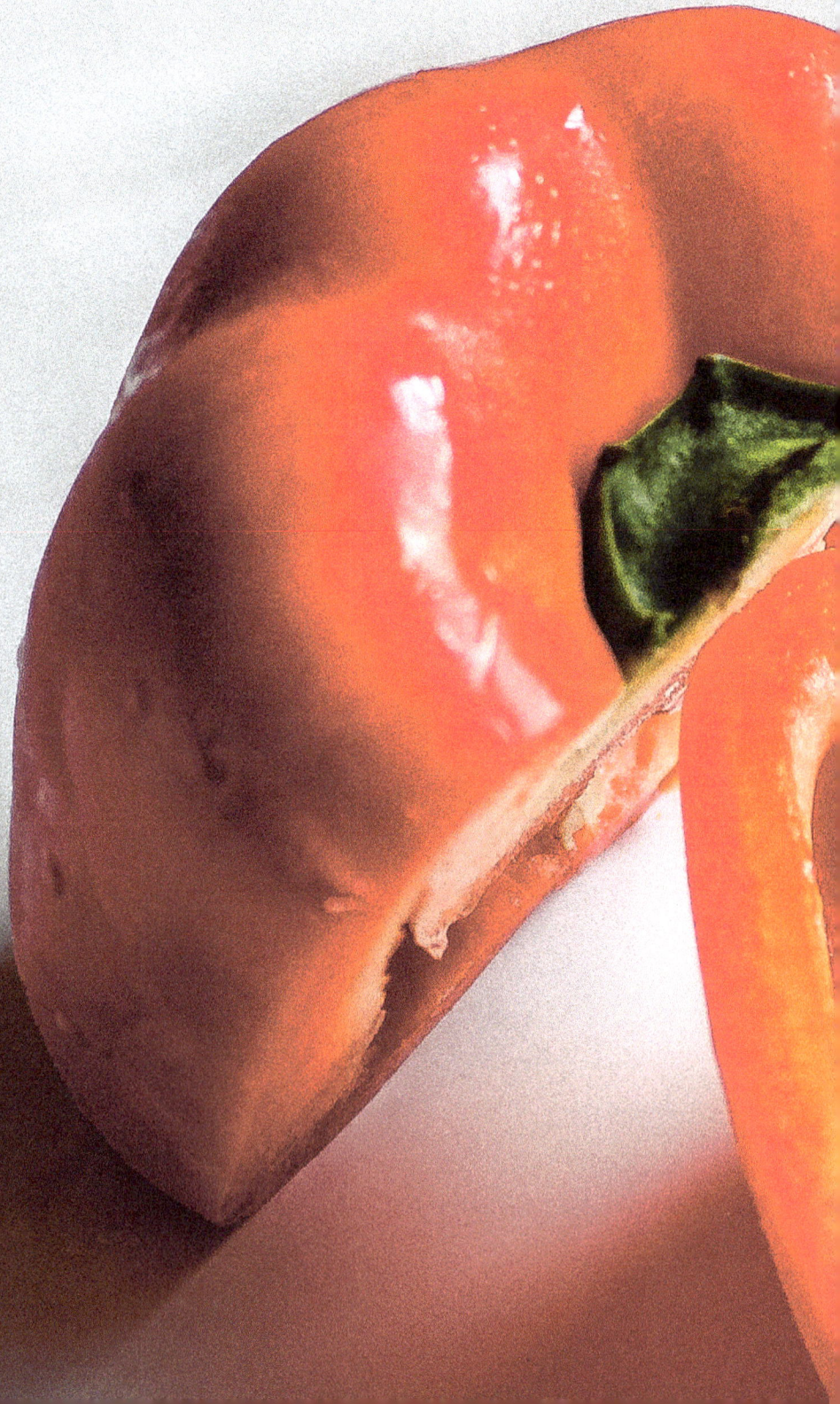

Culinary School

Culinary School: Week 2

June 8, 2016

This week marks my second week of culinary school and I'm pumped to check in with y'all to share a few things I'm learning. First off, it feels great to be a student again. Wearing a backpack and buying school supplies has been a fun transition.

Though I haven't had the opportunity to roll up my sleeves and get in the kitchen yet, I'm taking two lecture-heavy classes this semester: (1) Principles of Culinary Leadership and (2) Safety & Sanitation. I am super interested in the course content and my classes have been ripe with enlightening discussion. I really like my professor, Chef Alex (pronounced Ah-lex); I have her for both courses. Originally from Northern California, she went to culinary school in Atlanta and has her Master of Education degree. She's funny and often shares real life scenarios from her experience working in the field.

In Principles of Culinary Leadership, we explore hospitality management techniques used in differing work environments with an emphasis on human relations, building a staff and leading a team. I find the material to be applicable to so many fields, not just culinary arts. I'm learning all about effective communication in the workplace, organizational flow charts, training and recruiting principles. Isn't it amazing that oftentimes in the workforce, we're thrown into management positions without proper training and expected to know this stuff? In so many industries, no wonder the turnover rate is so high, and the wrong people are in the wrong roles! The entire team suffers under poor management. I could write a book on this topic from personal experience. It's amazing to be taught the keys to supervisory success and the components of management. There really is a method to the madness!

Good news: I got a 100 on my first homework assignment. Also, for our class project, each student must create a handbook for a fictitious hospitality organization. In class this week, we discussed the first component of the project – our mission statement. Would you like to see what I came up with? It was so fun letting my mind wander about what kind of restaurant I would own, if I were to open one someday. I took inspiration from one of my favorite coastal Southern dining spots–Barbara Jean's, and made it my own.

Rebekah Anne's

Coastal Country-Chic Cooking

Mission Statement

Founded in 2016, Rebekah Anne's is the destination for refined Southern dining and innovative cocktails on Georgia's beautiful coast. Fresh seafood, classic down-home dishes and Southern hospitality meet in this oceanfront restaurant where guests are treated like family and excellence is the standard upon every visit. With each meal, our knowledgeable staff confidently delivers consistent service. We believe in sourcing quality ingredients locally and serving a seasonal, ever-changing menu. We take pride in offering live music every weekend and a beachside dance floor where memories are made to last a lifetime.

How'd I do? It needs a little work, but I was encouraged after reading my idea aloud in class when the first comment from one of my peers was, "When are you opening?" followed by agreement and laughter. Two of my classmates even asked me for help with their own. Thumbs up!

My Safety & Sanitation class is one of those foundation classes students must take before they can move on to any of the other coursework. We're learning fundamental kitchen and dining room safety, sanitation, maintenance and operation procedures. I'm excited to understand how to operate and clean large-scale equipment and about knife safety. Stock, soup and sauce production is also covered. Upon completion of this class, I'll be ServSafe certified. Accredited by the American National Standards Institute, the sanitation certification is required by most restaurants as a basic credential for management staff. In layman's terms, I'll be legit, y'all!

As my second week of culinary school comes to a close, there are two things this Georgia girl has figured out. In response to my instructors, I've replaced the phrase "Yes ma'am" and "Yes sir" with a lively "Yes CHEF!" I've realized too, that all my curly hair can indeed fit into a chef's hat. That's a relief!

Until next time, I've got some studying to do. I'm off to create flashcards on foodborne illnesses and cross-contamination.

Knife Skills, Gardening and Looking the Part: My First Semester of Culinary School

July 20, 2016

In just two weeks, I'll have under my belt my first semester of culinary school. I've never been more interested to learn. In the classroom and the kitchen, I'm like a ravenous animal, hungry for every crumb of knowledge I can swallow. Already, my mind has been exposed to so many new concepts: I've been introduced to French words and techniques like "Tourne" and "Concasse," each referring to a different classic knife cut. In response to my instructors, I've replaced the phrase "Yes ma'am" and "Yes sir" with a lively "Yes Chef!"

During my first few days getting ready for school, I felt as though I was dressing up in a costume of sorts, but routine has found me comfortably accustomed to my uniform. For every class I dress in full brigade: a white chef's hat and double-breasted jacket with checked black and white pants. I wear black non-slip shoes, matching socks and a white apron. No jewelry is allowed, and my fingernails must be kept short.

Along with the experience I'm gaining, comes a whole new world of networking opportunities and a serious appreciation for the creative and diverse field of culinary arts. Going to culinary school once meant graduating and going to work in a kitchen, but today, with the boom of food media and entertainment, there are so many exciting paths one can take. Many of my classmates want to open their own bakeries and food trucks. My goal is to combine my education and background in marketing, public relations and writing with my culinary degree to ultimately host my own cooking television show, highlighting Georgia farmers and local restaurateurs. I would also love to be a food editor for a leading magazine and to have a few cookbooks of my own. As a recipe often needs an extra pinch of salt, culinary school will provide me with just the right touch of credibility to help me achieve the outcome I'm going after.

Of the classes I'm taking this summer, Principles of Culinary Leadership is primarily lecture, while Safety & Sanitation has a little lecture combined with hands-on time in the kitchen. In culinary leadership, we explore hospitality management techniques used in differing work environments with an emphasis on human relations, building a staff and leading a team. I find the material to be applicable to so many fields, not just culinary arts. I'm learning all about effective communication in the workplace, training and recruiting principles and supervisory skills in a professional kitchen. For our class project, we have to create an employee handbook including all the components we've learned. It's been fun to allow my mind to wander while imagining my fictitious restaurant. There are days we visit the school garden to pull weeds and to study the fruit and vegetable producing plants too.

My Safety & Sanitation class is one of those foundational classes students must take before they can move on to any of the other coursework. We're learning fundamental kitchen and dining room safety, sanitation, maintenance and operation procedures. At the end of this class, I'm looking forward to taking my ServSafe Certification exam, which will cover a few topics like foodborne illnesses, time-temperature abuse and cross contamination. As my knowledge has increased, I've become more aware of the way I do things in my home kitchen too, such as thawing chicken or reheating and cooling leftovers. Now, my husband jokingly says there's no living with me.

Cleaning is a large part of culinary school, and I'd be telling a fib if I didn't say there's a great deal of scrubbing the deck, cleaning and sanitizing your work surfaces and knowing which work areas, cutting boards and utensils to use for which task. It was Albert Einstein who said, "The more I learn, the more I realize how much I don't know." He was spot on, and knowledge truly is power.

Next semester, I'll really get to roll up my sleeves and get my apron dirty. I'm taking Principles of Cooking in addition to Principles of Baking and I can hardly wait. If you'd like to keep up with my culinary school journey, be sure to follow my food blog by visiting *SomeKindaGood.com* or connect with *Some Kinda Good* on social media. Let's share cooking experiences and talk food. You may even find a recipe or two worth cooking.

Cooking and Baking My Way Through Culinary School

September 8, 2016

My second semester of culinary school is moving at an exciting pace. I'm finally beginning to feel comfortable in the professional kitchen, getting my bearings and learning how to use the large-scale equipment. I'm taking two classes this fall: Principles of Cooking and Principles of Baking, and my two books together weigh nearly 13 pounds! Would you believe I've already gotten my first kitchen "scar?" It was a total rookie mistake.

When tasting for seasonings a blonde roux, that is, equal parts butter and flour cooked to the proper color and used to thicken sauces, I became so enamored with the texture and color of the thickener, that I completely dismissed the fact that the stockpot had just come from a medium-heat gas flame. Excited that my group's roux had reached the proper consistency, with my finger I swiped the back of my stirring spoon for a quick taste. Ouch! My memory returned immediately when my skin touched the hot concoction and I may or may not have lost my religion right there next to the stove.

Over the past three weeks, my cooking class has covered stocks, soups and stews. From scratch, we've made chicken, veal and fish stocks with a Sachet d'Epices which literally translates, bag of spices. Parsley stems, bay leaves, fresh thyme and peppercorns are wrapped in a small cheesecloth sack and secured with kitchen twine, tied to the handle of the pot and draped directly over the side and into the liquid. The herbs and spices add an earthy depth of flavor to an otherwise bland stock.

I've learned to cook the five French mother sauces: Bechamel (white sauce), Espagnole (brown sauce), Tomato, Hollandaise and Veloute (blonde sauce). With each sauce, we prepare a complimentary protein or starch for two purposes: to taste all the components together and to practice plating. When working in the kitchen, our class of about 16 students is split into groups of four. Each group is tasked with a deadline of presenting a plate to be critiqued on flavor, visual interest and portion size by our instructor.

With the fresh tomato sauce, we used eggplant and basil from our garden, and made large batches of eggplant parmesan. With the Espagnole, we grilled pork and served the brown sauce right over the top. With our Bechamel, a milk-based sauce

From left: Laney Golden, Rebekah and other culinary school classmates

thickened with a white roux, we added fresh cheeses thereby creating a derivative of Bechamel called Mornay, then tossed the creamy sauce with al dente penne pasta. The Hollandaise, an emulsion of egg yolk and liquid butter whisked into submission, was beautiful over Eggs Benedict: toasted bread, pan-fried ham and a perfectly cooked poached egg. I am satisfied to say, my instructor, Executive Chef Alex, said my group produced a "perfect" Eggs Benedict. Our Espagnole sauce over grilled pork was best in class. As for the Bechamel with pasta, we garnished our dish with a whole sprig of parsley instead of chopping it and Chef Alex commented, "1980 called and wants their garnish back." I guess you can't win them all.

While Tropical Storm Hermine canceled week two of my Principles of Baking class, we've already baked soft white dinner rolls and cracked wheat bread with dried cranberries. The process of activating fresh yeast, mixing it in batter and waiting for dough to double in size is quite fun. Pounding out the dough is a sure stress reliever, and rolling it to the proper smoothness is truly an art. After that comes proofing, then scoring and finally baking. Bread knots have also been an enlightening exercise. With dough, I now know how to execute a single, double and three-braid knot. We eat with our eyes first and presentation makes all the difference. My instructor, Chef Szabo, says, "Baking is a science and a chemistry. That's what makes us different."

Over the summer, I came out on top of my classes with straight A's. I even made the Dean's List and passed my National Restaurant Association ServSafe Certification exam. I'm hoping to keep that momentum going this semester, with all my fingers intact.

Finals and Finishing Strong

December 5, 2016

By the time you're reading this, I'll have just one week of finals to go before I complete my second semester of culinary school. Finals week marks the end of the most rigorous 16-week schedule I've experienced yet, and come December 9, it will be time to celebrate!

There are days I love what I'm learning and trying days when I must remind myself of my goals. Make no mistake: Culinary school is backbreaking work and manual labor. The job is very physical: standing for extended periods of time, lifting, bending and stirring mass quantities. These days, I'm feeling every bit of my 33 years of age, and the more I learn about the food industry, the more I realize just how important it is to have a passion for the field.

In my Principles of Cooking class, I've had several good moments, but my journey this semester has not been without its failures. I've scorched Béchamel sauce and had to begin again, seared my chicken breast on the wrong side and served undercooked rice. However, with every failure, I'm seeing the error of my ways and refining my skill.

Last week in preparation for a large-scale event hosted by my college, I was tasked with making 18 gallons of tomato bisque. I never want to see another tomato for as long as I live. At the beginning of class, my Chef Instructor assigned me the bisque, then asked, "Do you need any helpers?" I thought, "It's tomato soup; how hard could it be?" This was before I scaled out the recipe or realized the amount I had to prepare. So, I said, "No, I should be able to handle it." WRONG. When I tell you this soup took as long to prep as it did to cook, I am not kidding! During the process, thank goodness some of my trusty classmates stepped in to help. The ingredients alone included six pounds of onion, three pounds

each of celery and carrot, 72 minced garlic cloves, 54 quarts of homemade chicken stock, 10 pounds of roux and 63 pounds of tomatoes—all of which I had to open with a hand-crank style can opener, then strain. To stir the pot, I climbed a step ladder, and used the largest immersion blender I've ever seen for blending all the ingredients together (it was quite fun to use a power tool of that magnitude!). While I was "in the weeds" so to speak, whisking the 10 pounds of roux (that's equal parts butter and flour) with all my might, sweat beading on my forehead as I stood over the gas burners, I looked at my instructor and said with gusto, "Culinary school will make a man out of me yet, or I will quickly realize this is not for me!" The good news is, the tomato bisque turned out delicious, despite my need to take a muscle relaxer the next day.

I am working physically harder than I've ever worked but am convinced I am a better cook now than I was when I began.

For my final this Tuesday, there are two parts, one written and the other is our practical. There are four things I must produce for the practical within an allotted time frame: 1) A plate with four components–protein, starch, vegetable and sauce, 2) A fabricated (butchered) whole chicken, 3) Homemade chicken stock and 4) Demonstration of specific knife skills. Our plate must reveal the techniques we've learned such as knife skills, searing and blanching. We're graded on a number of factors: plating presentation, flavor, texture and temperature of the dish, consistency of sauce, professionalism in the kitchen and what we refer to in the culinary industry as "mise en place" or everything in its place. I'm feeling prepared and a little nervous, but I know with hustle, focus and organization, I will get the job done and done well.

Pretty soon, I'll be decorating my Christmas tree and sipping on a festive libation. Until then, as I aim to finish 2016 strong, y'all be sure to send good vibes my way. Follow along on my culinary school journey by connecting with *Some Kinda Good* on social media. Good food and good company, that's what it's all about!

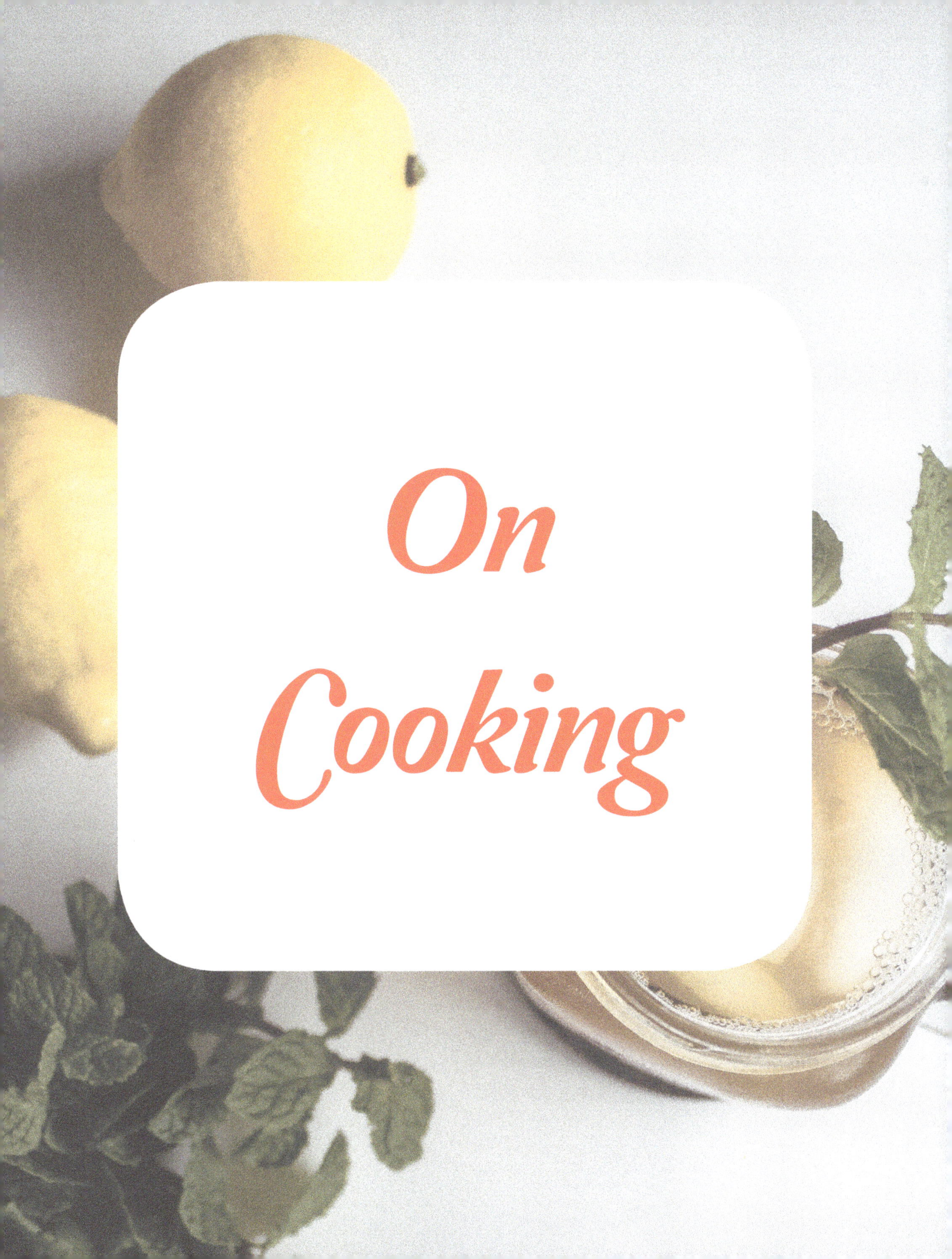

On Cooking

Crack This:
Farm Eggs vs. Store Bought

May 22, 2013

I've eaten eggs from the grocery store my entire life. I'm sure at some point in my childhood I've tasted an egg fresh from the chicken coop because my Grandpa raised chickens, but that was before my palate was experienced enough to appreciate the difference. It's true that when you've never experienced better, you don't know what you're missing.

So, when my good lookin' boyfriend showed up at my door last week with one dozen, light brown and cream-colored farm eggs in one hand and a beautiful bouquet of flowers in the other (I know...keeper), I set my sights on cooking the eggs just the way a farmer recommended: in a little bacon grease with salt and pepper. I've never tasted anything like these eggs... it was pure eggstacy (had to do it!). Seriously, the flavor is out of this world, and sure to make you crack a smile (okay, okay). During cooking I found them to be fluffier than a store-bought egg. Produced by free-range chickens, farm eggs are more nutritious because the chickens can roam freely and eat a natural diet. They contain no added hormones or fillers and are not processed.

One meal that exemplifies comfort food for me and really lets the farm egg shine, is the tried and true bacon, egg and cheese sandwich. A fancy meal has its time and place, but it's not always the five-star, fine dining plates that trip my trigger.

138

Sometimes, a good ol' familiar meal is the only thing I need to feel centered, satisfied and one with my kitchen again. Served with a side of cheese grits, breakfast for dinner has never been better.

And remember, when building the sandwich, it's all about good architecture. Somehow, the sandwich tastes better when cut into a triangle shape too. At least, that's the way mama always sent me to school, with a neatly packed cut-in-half sandwich in my brown paper sack.

Bacon, Egg and Cheese Biscuit

Serves 1

- Thick cut, hickory smoked bacon
- Honey Wheat Bread, such as Nature's Own
- 2 farm fresh chicken eggs
- Blackberry jelly, such as Smucker's (or a batch from your local farmers' market!)
- Sharp cheddar cheese, sliced

Cook three strips of bacon in a skillet on medium heat until just crispy. Remove from the pan and drain on paper towels. Pour off some of the grease, reserving enough to cook the eggs, about 1 - 2 tablespoons. Whisk the eggs together in a small bowl, season with salt and pepper. Pour the eggs into the pan and let set. Cook for about 2 -3 minutes on each side, flipping once for even browning. Meanwhile, slice or grate the cheddar cheese and toast two slices of bread. Spread toasted bread with blackberry jelly, then build the sandwich.

Strawberry Basil Sauce and How to Use It

May 27, 2018

Strawberry season is officially here and if you've visited your local farmers' market lately, you know exactly what I mean. After a trip to the Forsyth Farmers' Market over the weekend, I brought home a gallon-sized bucket full of farm-picked, red-ripened strawberries and developed the most luscious and sweet sauce oozing with strawberry flavor. Paired with fresh basil from my garden and a hint of lemon juice, the sauce comes together in minutes and can be used in so many ways!

ome Kinda Good Strawberry-Basil Sauce

The cornstarch helps the sauce to thicken, resulting in a velvety smooth finish, while the acidity from the lemon juice cuts the sweetness slightly, balancing the flavors.

Place strawberries and sugar in a large stockpot over medium-high heat and bring to a boil, stirring to combine. Add cornstarch slurry and reduce temperature to medium-low. Allow the sauce to cook and thicken for about 10 minutes. Remove from heat and let cool slightly. Carefully pour the sauce into a food processor or blender, adding lemon juice, zest, salt and basil. Pulse to desired consistency.

Here are a few other ideas on how to use my Strawberry-Basil Sauce:

- Pour it over cold vanilla ice cream

- Add rum and make a strawberry daiquiri

- Pour it into ice cube trays and freeze for a flavorful addition to any drink

Four Techniques for Boosting Flavor in Stocks, Sauces and Soups

October 9, 2016

When the air turns crisp and the evenings become dark earlier, a comforting and flavorful soup or slow-simmering stew on the stovetop is a welcome way to bring calm to a busy day's end. Served alongside a bright salad and a crusty loaf of Italian bread, the warmth and aromas of a good soup throughout the home can heal and soothe, like food for the soul.

Today, I'm sharing four cooking techniques that will add tons of flavor to your stocks, sauces and soups. Standard Bouquet Garni, Sachet D'Epices, Oignon Brule and Oignon Pique are traditional French aromatic preparations called for again and again in recipes. Meant to enhance and support the flavors of a dish, they add subtle undertones of earthiness to stocks, sauces and soups by gently infusing the liquid with their aroma. Try one of these techniques next time you set out to make a stock from scratch or a pot of soup, and your friends and family are sure to be impressed.

You'll need some kitchen twine and cheesecloth. You can find these at craft stores, such as Michael's or Hobby Lobby.

1   Standard Bouquet Garni

A bouquet garni, literally translated garnished bouquet, is made up of fresh herbs and vegetables tied into a bundle. Rinse leek leaves thoroughly, then use the leek leaves as a base for

stacking and wrapping the remaining ingredients. Tie a piece of kitchen twine around the bundle and be sure to cut a piece of string long enough to tie the bouquet to the pot handle for easy removal. Note: Parsley leaves are stripped from the stems because they will impart unwanted color in your dish. You can always chop them up and use for garnish. Ingredients include:

- 1 sprig of fresh thyme

- 3 or 4 parsley stems

- 1 bay leaf

- 2 or 3 leek leaves and/or 1 celery stalk, cut lengthwise

- 1 carrot, cut in half lengthwise (optional)

- 1 parsnip, cut in half lengthwise (optional)

2   Sachet D'Epices

Sachet D'Epices (pronounced "sa-SHAY DAY-pees") translates to bag of spices. Containing ingredients that would otherwise get lost in the sauce so to speak, such as peppercorns, cheesecloth is used to form a makeshift sack. Bundle the ingredients in a small rectangle of cheesecloth and secure the sack by tying it together with kitchen twine. As with the garnished bouquet, be sure to cut a piece of string long enough to tie the sachet to the pot handle for easy removal. Drop the sachet directly into the pot. Ingredients include:

- 3 or 4 parsley stems

- 1 sprig thyme or 1 tsp dried thyme

- 1 bay leaf

- 1 teaspoon cracked peppercorns

- 1 garlic clove (optional)

For small batch soups, stocks and sauces (less than one gallon), sachets and bouquets should be added in the last 15 to 30 minutes of cooking. For batches of several gallons or more, add it about one hour before the end of the cooking time.

3 Oignon Brule

The Oignon Brule has got to be my favorite technique. Translated "burnt onion," an Oignon Brule is made by peeling and halving an onion and charring the cut faces in a dry skillet. This may be the one time that it's okay to burn something intentionally while you're cooking! This technique is used in some stocks to provide golden brown color. I've used it while preparing vegetable stock, and the outcome was delightful. Peel an onion, slice it in half, then place both halves face down in a dry skillet over high heat. If you have a gas oven, the onion may be placed directly on the flame. Be sure to burn the onion halves until they are black. Place the burnt onions directly in the pot while your soup, sauce or stock simmers. Remove when the dish has finished cooking.

4 Oignon Pique

Oignon Pique or "pricked" or "studded onion" is prepared by studding an onion with a few whole cloves and a bay leaf. Attach one or more bay leaves to an onion by pushing whole cloves through the leaves into the onion (like thumb tacks). Much like with the Oignon Brule, the Oignon Pique is added directly to simmering liquid during the cooking process.

Try these techniques with recipes on *SomeKindaGood.com*! You'll find lots of inspiration there like my Hearty Hamburger and Roasted Root Vegetable soups, and Wild Georgia Shrimp and Corn Chowder. It was French Chef Louis P. De Gouy who said, "Good soup is one of the prime ingredients of good living. For soup can do more to lift the spirits and stimulate the appetite than any other one dish."

How to Create Garlic-Herb Flavored Butter

January 12, 2016

I love quick cooking tips that pack big flavor punch! Today, we're talking butter...that little stick of happiness that literally makes *everything* better. Julia Child said it herself: "With enough butter, anything is good." For a cook, room temperature butter is like a blank canvas. If you've never tried flavored butters, they're really great for enhancing bread, sandwiches, seafood, chicken and even steaks. They make even the most mundane meal special. As if butter could get any better, right? Today, I'm sharing a three-ingredient recipe for garlic-herb butter that will take bread from basic to gourmet in minutes.

If you're anything like me, it's often you end up with leftover or day-old baguette. I can never seem to use the entire thing! I bought a loaf of French bread for the purpose of making bruschetta the other day, and when I was finished, there sat over half a loaf. So, when spaghetti was the main course for dinner the next day, the softened butter in my dish on the countertop held all the more appeal. What better side dish to round out the meal than with crusty slices of garlic-herb bread? With half a stick of my room temperature butter in a bowl, I simply minced one large clove of garlic, chopped about 3 - 4 tablespoons of parsley and added a pinch of sea salt. You can use any combination of fresh herbs you have on hand. Thyme, basil, you name it. If you'd like to try the same thing, here's how: Using a serrated knife, slice the French loaf right down the center, place the halves on a large baking sheet and prepare it for slathering.

Smear the butter mixture all over the bread, taking extra care to get the mixture into all those little crevices. Pop the pan in the oven and bake at 425 degrees for 10 minutes. When the bread has finished baking, the garlic looks as if it has attained the ultimate tan. The combination of the garlic and herb mixture makes your home smell like a neighborhood bakery. Tucked next to a plate of spaghetti, the garlic-herb bread makes the meal *Some Kinda Good*.

Flavored butters can be sweet or savory. Here are a few other recipe ideas to pair with softened butter:

- Local honey and a pinch of salt for serving with hot biscuits

- Chopped fresh blackberries, jam or pear preserves for serving with homemade bread

- Cajun spices for serving with grilled shrimp

The possibilities are endless.

Sunday Supper Edition: Herb Roasted Chicken

February 26, 2017

The warm climate we experience in Southeast Georgia often leaves cold temperatures few and far between. It's only February and already, I've had my first beach day of 2017. On the days when the cooler temperatures do decide to come our way, there's one recipe that I turn to again and again: Herb Roasted Chicken in my cast iron skillet. A meal steaming hot and full of flavor, it cooks all at once in one dish. Clean-up is easy, and the flavors are so earthy, warm and soul-satisfying. Roast chicken is simple enough to prepare for family on a weeknight, but also impressive enough to serve to company. My husband and I recently had another couple over for a small dinner party, and I made roast chicken with crispy Brussels sprouts and red potatoes. Everyone raved about it and still asks for the recipe. Roasting is one of the most flavorful techniques in cooking, and when executed well, the sky is the limit.

Today I'm sharing my recipe for Herb Roasted Chicken with you. The vegetables you choose to roast with the chicken are versatile, as are the seasonings and fat used on the bird. Some recipes use olive oil and others softened butter. Both are effective for producing a crisp skin. Make my recipe just the way it is or use it as a guide and substitute the flavors you enjoy most. Cooking is all about experimenting and I hope you'll do just that.

I love cooking with my cast iron skillet, but if you don't have one, feel free to use a roasting pan or a glass 9 x 13 dish for this recipe.

The skin of the chicken gets crispy and golden brown and the vegetables soak up all the juices, making this meal the most tender, comfort food feast. Meanwhile, your entire home will beckon neighbors with its enticing aroma. Serve this for Sunday supper for an extra special sit-down meal with the family.

The important thing to remember when cooking chicken is to understand that poultry must be cooked to an internal temperature of 165 degrees to be safe to eat. Be sure to temp your meat before you eat!

Herb Roasted Chicken

Dress the bird by squeezing the juice of half a lemon over the outside, then place the other half of the lemon inside the cavity of the chicken. Next, slather the bird with olive oil and season it liberally with salt, pepper and dried herbs. If possible, dress the bird a day in advance, and when you're ready to cook it the next day, remove it from the refrigerator and allow it to reach room temperature before roasting.

Make a "bird nest" in your cast iron skillet by piling the chopped vegetables in the center. Season them with salt and pepper and toss them all together with a teaspoon of olive oil. Perch the bird on the top, breast side up. Pour ½ cup of chicken stock into the pan. Roast in a 375-degree oven for 1 hour and 20 to 30 minutes. Before serving, allow the bird to rest 5 to 10 minutes. Remove the chicken from the vegetables and turn the oven up to 400 degrees. Roast the vegetables in the pan for about 10 minutes, until they are browned and crispy on top.

If desired, make a pan gravy with the drippings. Remove the vegetables from the skillet and keep warm. Add 2 tablespoons of flour to the drippings and cook on medium heat, scraping the browned bits from the bottom of the pan. Slowly whisk in a cup of chicken stock and stir until thickened, seasoning with salt and pepper to taste. Add more stock if needed. Add two tablespoons of butter and stir until it melts. Serve over rice, alongside the roasted chicken and vegetables.

Three Practical Ways to Cook with Fresh Herbs

March 5, 2017

One Saturday afternoon recently while cleaning out the shed, my husband and I came across several Terra Cotta clay pots left behind by the previous dwellers of our new Savannah home. I've never been one to plant or garden, but I knew if I used them for anything, I would want to plant something I could cook with, something that would enhance the flavor of food. Buying individual packages of fresh herbs in the grocery store can be costly, and when compared with the cost of growing them yourself, the decision is a no-brainer! A visit to my local home and garden store revealed fresh herbs on sale and a weekend project was born.

I filled each pot with a mixture of equal parts moisture control potting mix and composted cow manure. Then, I followed package directions and planted each herb carefully.

Though I'm not an experienced green thumb, I *have* been cooking with fresh herbs for some time. Let's talk about a few inspired ways to use them and how they can take meals from simple to *Some Kinda Good*!

My new herb "garden" includes basil (a must!), thyme, mint, flat leaf parsley, Italian oregano and cilantro. I chose these six herbs because I cook with them the most often. **Basil** is delicious on paninis (grilled sandwiches) and pizza; **thyme** when combined with melted butter makes a great splash for finishing seared steaks; **mint** is a must-have in a tall, cold glass of freshly-brewed sweet iced tea; **parsley** makes any casserole, seafood or sauce brighter with its pop of green color; **oregano** makes a fantastic pesto or flavor booster for roast chicken; and finally, **cilantro** is perfect for tacos, guacamole and Mexican casseroles.

In addition to these ideas, here are my top three practical applications for using fresh herbs in the kitchen.

1   Compound Butters

Fresh herbs are great for making flavorful compound butters, both sweet and savory. A compound butter is simply an ingredient added to softened butter that acts as an instant sauce for meats, vegetables and fish, or as a sweet topping on breads, pancakes or baked goods. Have you ever been to a restaurant where they served a variety of softened butters to slather on top of warm, freshly baked bread? Whipped honey butter with cinnamon or savory options, like this garlic-herb butter are my favorites.

2   Sachet d'Epices or Bouquet Garni

As many of you know, I'm a food columnist for the Statesboro Herald, a 6-day daily publication in Southeast Georgia. In one recent column, "4 Techniques for Boosting Flavor in Stocks, Sauces" I include the classical French techniques for Sachet d'Epices (Bag of Spices) and a Bouquet Garni (Garnished Bouquet)–aromatic preparations called for again and again in recipes. Meant to enhance and support the flavors of a dish, they add subtle undertones of earthiness to stocks, sauces and soups by gently infusing the liquid with their aroma. Fresh herbs are a key ingredient!

3 Garnish

One of the most popular and practical uses for fresh herbs is garnishing gravy, sauces, desserts or casseroles. Take a look at how adding minced parsley to brown onion gravy makes it that much more appealing. The slideshow below also shows off beautifully finished plates. A proper garnish is like the perfect accessory to an outfit. We eat with our eyes first!

Tasty Ways to Cook with Venison

January 28, 2018

Deer season ended in early January, and thanks to the hunting skills of my good-looking husband, Kurt, we've got a freezer full of venison: ground and stew meat, cubed steak and sausage. I've only recently begun cooking with venison, and up until about two years ago, I hadn't eaten much of it in my lifetime. When Kurt got his first deer around Thanksgiving in 2016, I suddenly found myself with 40 pounds of Middle Georgia doe, and it was time to learn how to cook it. Good thing I did, because this season brought two more deer: a 6-point buck on Veteran's Day and another doe on the last weekend of hunting season. At first, I wasn't sure I'd like it. I'd heard folks say it tastes "gamey," and I wasn't quite sure what to expect. Well, I'm here to tell you: When a deer is handled properly, there is nothing gamey about the taste.

Good tasting deer meat has to do with several factors. One of the most primary being, you must let it bleed out for a couple of days before taking it to the processor. Good venison needs to age. After the deer has been cleaned and skinned, place a layer of ice on the bottom of your cooler, then place the meat on top of that and top it with more ice. Place the cooler outdoors in a shady spot, pointed downhill with the drain plug open. This purges the blood from the meat and keeps it cool.

Cooking with ground venison is much like cooking with ground beef. It can be substituted for most any ground beef recipe. The same goes for the other cuts of meat. If you know how to make country fried steak, you can just as easily make country fried venison. If you know how to make beef stew, you can just as easily make venison stew. You get the idea. When it comes to grilling steaks or the backstrap portion of a deer, do not overcook it. Deer is most flavorful and juicy when cooked medium rare.

The other day on my Instagram account, @SKGFoodBlog, I posted a mouthwatering photo of my garlic and herb venison penne pasta with homemade tomato sauce. I had prepared the dish in my cast iron skillet. The first comment I received was from a Statesboro local who said, "That looks amazing and I am always looking for recipes that use venison!" With another deer season behind us, I figured there were a few more of you who might like some deer dinner ideas. Try making these dishes at home, and for more inspiration in the kitchen, be sure to visit Somekindagood.com.

- Venison Rigatoni

- Venison Stew

- Country Fried Venison

- Grilled Venison Backstrap

- Venison Vegetable Lasagna

- Venison chili

Venison Stew

Serves 8

Ingredients

- 2 lbs of venison stew meat, cubed
- 1 cup all-purpose flour
- 1 tbsp garlic salt
- 1 tbsp cayenne pepper
- 1 tbsp Herbs de Provence
- 4 slices of hardwood smoked, thick-cut bacon, clipped into pieces
- 1 medium Vidalia onion, diced
- 3 celery stalks, sliced
- 3 carrots, peeled and diagonally sliced
- 1 medium red bell pepper, chopped
- 1 large clove of garlic, minced
- Extra virgin olive oil, if needed
- Salt and pepper
- 4 cups beef broth
- 1 cup dry red wine, such as Cabernet Sauvignon
- Bay leaf
- 3 sprigs of fresh thyme and 3 sprigs of parsley, plus more for garnish

Special equipment needed

- Large Dutch oven, such as Le Creuset
- 1 gallon sandwich bag

Cooking with ground venison is much like cooking with ground beef. It can be substituted for most any ground beef recipe. This venison stew recipe is hearty and filling, and warms you up after a long day of hunting in the stand. It's also great for a good weeknight family dinner. Flavored with fresh herbs from my garden and rich beef broth, I like to serve it with crusty, buttered French bread and a side salad.

In a 1-gallon Zip Lock bag or paper sack, place the flour, garlic salt, cayenne pepper and Herbs de Provence. Close the bag and shake well to combine the seasonings and flour. Add the meat to the bag. Close it and shake well, turning the bag until all the pieces are well covered. Meanwhile, in a large Dutch oven over medium-high heat, cook bacon pieces until crispy, and set aside. With a set of tongs, shake off the excess flour from each piece of venison, adding it to the rendered bacon fat. Brown the meat on all sides, searing until a golden-brown crust develops. Turn the meat, every minute or so, until all sides have been browned. Remove the meat from the pan and set aside. Add a tablespoon of beef broth to the pan to deglaze it. Using a wooden spoon, loosen the bits from the bottom of the pan. Add the onion, celery, carrots, and bell pepper to the pan and sauté until tender, about five minutes. At this step, if your pan looks dry, add a few tablespoons of oil. Add the garlic and sauté for 30 seconds. Season well with salt and pepper. Return the venison to the pan and cover the meat and vegetables with the broth and red wine. Using kitchen twine, make a bundle with the thyme and parsley, tying a knot around the herbs and attaching the other end to the handle of the pot. Season again with salt and pepper. Cover the stew with a lid and bring to a boil. Reduce the heat to low and let simmer for 45 minutes to an hour. Taste the stew for seasoning and adjust as needed. Remove the bay leaves and discard the herb bundle. Garnish with fresh parsley and serve over rice.

Restaurant Reviews

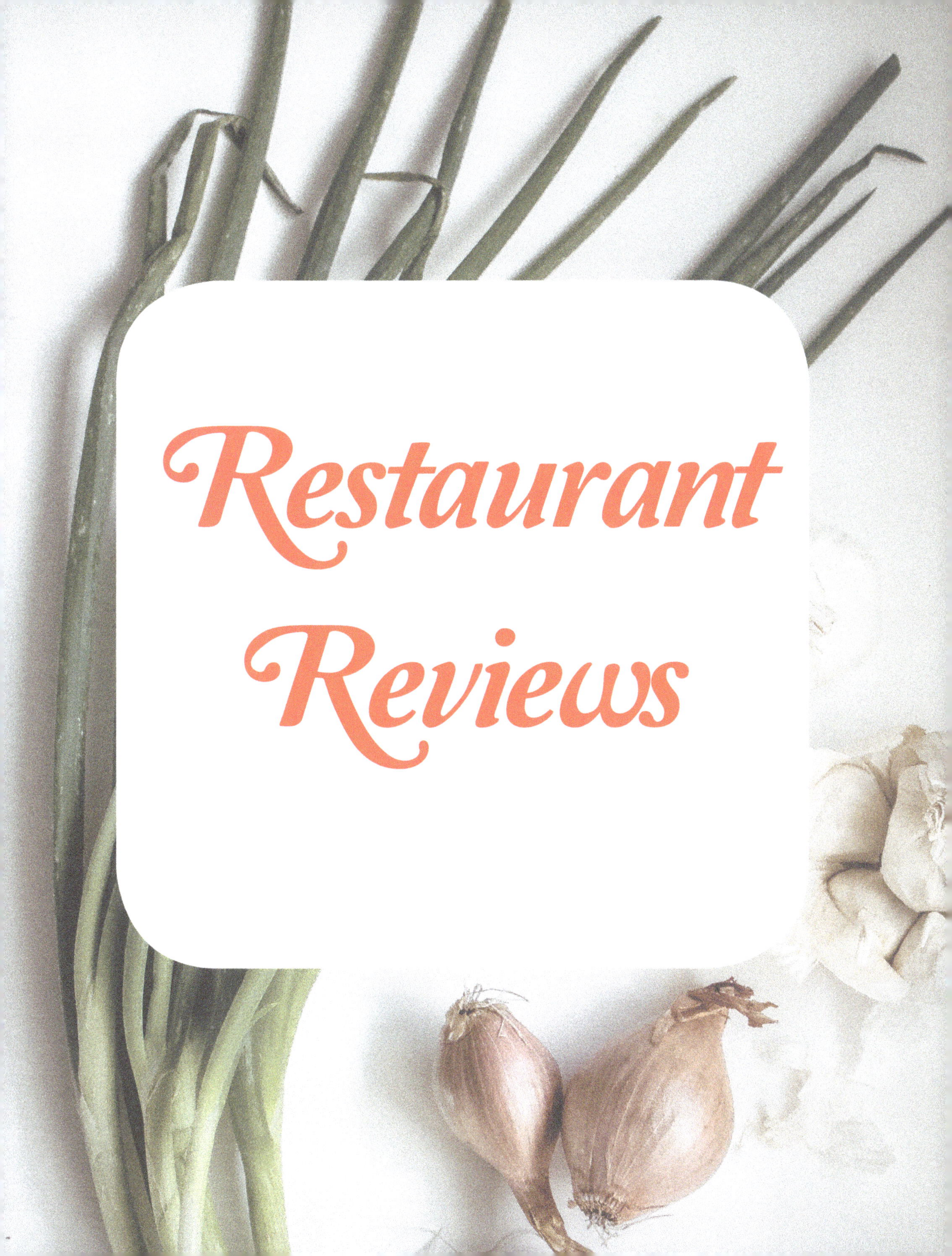

ATLANTA

Brunch in Buckhead: Watershed, a Southern Jewel

Watershed on Peachtree
July 22, 2013

Mornings and I have been butting heads since 1983–the year I was born. That's why brunch is quite possibly the best concept ever. I love everything about it. The idea that sleeping in is perfectly acceptable, the ease of drinking coffee in afternoon, the pleasure of indulging in breakfast and lunch foods simultaneously...it all feels a bit devious, but oh-so-good. When I roll to the big city of Atlanta, discovering new brunch spots is my tolerate-six-lane-traffic and fast-paced-people salvation. Upon my last visit, fate introduced me to Watershed on Peachtree. As if the complimentary valet parking wasn't enough, the country ham biscuits served with peach marmalade, local honey and whipped butter almost sent me over the edge. It's a Southern jewel with big presence, in a location where the competition is ravenous.

Recently named one of the Best New Restaurants in the American South by Conde Nast Traveler, the highfalutin' eatery is an upscale farm-to-table experience I believe everyone in the free world should try *at least* once. I ordered the Bay Bloody Mary, when I learned it was seasoned with Old Bay. Garnished with pickled green beans, pimento-stuffed olives and a juicy lime wedge, the souped-up cocktail and salted rim had me at hello.

Country ham is a rarity in restaurants anymore. To see it featured on the menu in its rightful place between two flaky,

fall-apart-in-your-mouth buttermilk biscuits...what is life? Other Starters on the brunch menu include Pimento Cheese Toast, Wild Mushroom Toast, Sausage Gravy & Biscuit served with bacon jam and fine herbs, and Smoked Ham Wrapped Gulf Shrimp a la plancha (grilled).

I'm attracted to all things coastal, even more so when I feel landlocked. Naturally, I ordered the Coconut Pancakes served with coconut syrup and a side of bacon. The bacon was cooked to perfection without an ounce of fat...lean and crispy, the perfect crunch to the meal. At just $10, the pancake stack was sweet and satisfying, keeping me full late into the day.

We also tried the Huevos Rancheros and Chilaquiles featuring eggs any style, Heywood's Andouille sausage and salsa ranchero. My boyfriend ordered a side of fries because the table's order next to us looked so appetizing. Potatoes rock. Offering a variety of sophisticated, yet recognizable dishes like Chicken Fried Poached Eggs, Seafood Melange and a Crabby Shrimp Burger, the brunch menu also boasts classics like the Southern Cobb and Wild Georgia Shrimp Salads. Prices range from $6.50 for Starters to $18.50 for Steak & Eggs.

Watershed on Peachtree has a beautiful, raw setting that's bright and open with modern lighting. From the moment you set foot in the elegant entryway, the cheerful and clean atmosphere invites you to stay.

Our server, John had been waiting tables at the restaurant for just four months but was very informative and most helpful. He told us all about the famous fried chicken served only on Wednesdays. In Southern Living magazine this month, Watershed on Peachtree is considered an upscale place to get The South's Best Fried Chicken, noting it's "always sold out by 8 p.m." He also shared that Executive Chef Joe Truex, native Louisianan, couldn't wait to begin serving up gumbo on Thursday nights.

Watershed on Peachtree has a commitment to seasonal, locally sourced ingredients. Many of the cocktails are even organic! With an ever-changing menu, the restaurant's cocktail napkins read, "creative and delicious Southern food enjoyed in comfort and community." I couldn't have said it better myself.

A Beach Food Experience for Landlocked Atlantans

The Optimist Fish Camp & Oyster Bar
March 11, 2013

I walked in and the first thing I saw were the words, "Country Ham" in navy blue and yellow, painted on a white wall. The restaurant had been converted from a previous slaughterhouse and the words preserved. Country ham is one of those Southern mainstays, and I knew immediately this was a place I would love. I had driven from the coastal plains of Southeast Georgia, about 200 miles, to the big city of Atlanta on a business trip to meet a good friend. We had done our research, and of all the fine places to dine in the notorious A-T-L, had naturally settled on what the restaurant's Twitter account classifies "A beach-food experience for landlocked Atlantans."

While we waited on our table in the main dining room, we sat at the Oyster Bar and tried just about everything–East and West coast oysters of every variety, snow crab & lobster knuckles, oyster crackers and salt & vinegar chips. The oysters were served with fresh horseradish and a mignonette sauce (a sauce of vinegar and shallots, typically served with raw oysters). The mignonette sauce was so bright and fresh, it would awaken even a sloth.

You can't have oysters without a cold beer, so I took the chance to try the one in a red can with a lighthouse pictured on the front—Cisco Brewers Sankaty Light from Nantucket, MA. The first oyster I tried was served over warm "coals," roasted in a wood-fired oven with parmesan cheese and bacon. It was one of the most beautiful things I've ever seen. The Opi Salt &

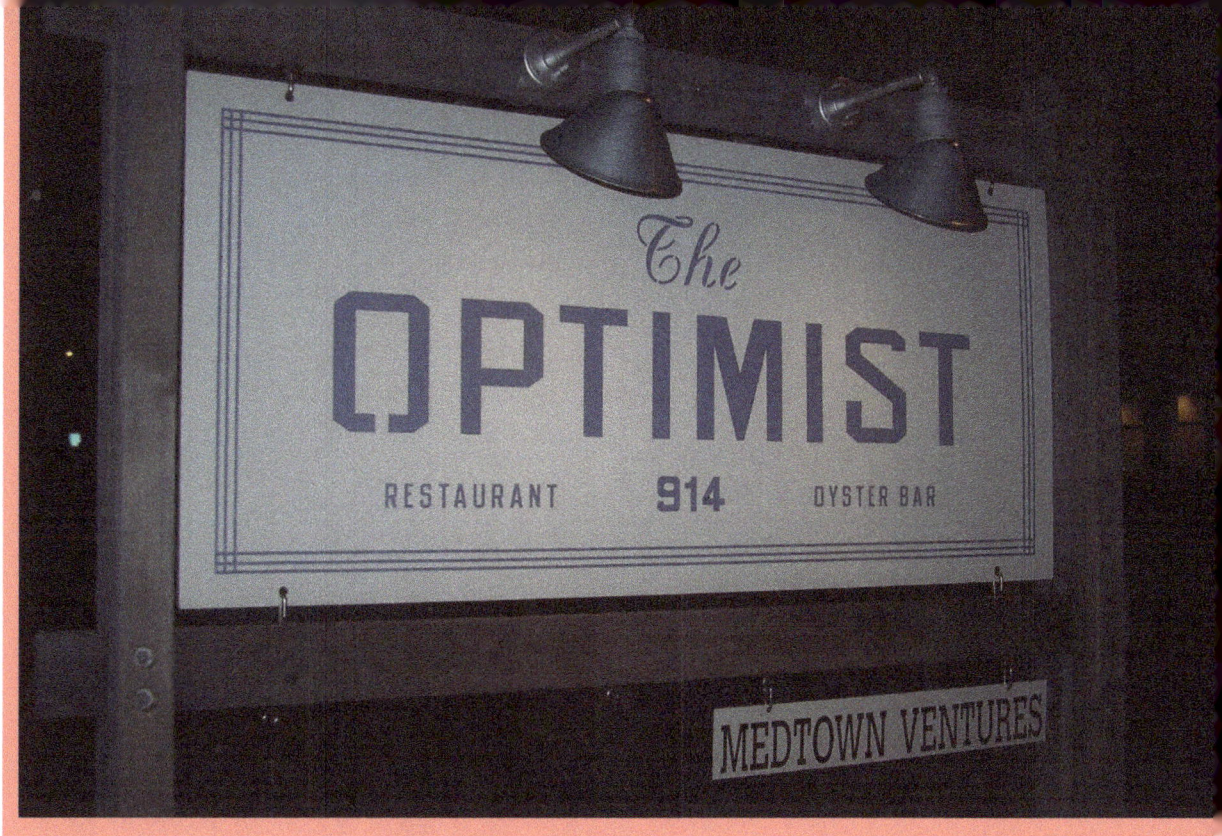

Vinegar Chips were crunchy...the perfect bar food. Next, let's talk about the snow crab claw & lobster knuckles in a chili-lime butter bath. It took a little work, but once I got my hands on the cracking tool, we were good to go.

I experienced food at The Optimist like I have never experienced food before...intense flavors with no detail undone when it came to presentation. Every encounter I had with staff members was pleasant, from the hostess taking notice of my black dress and providing me a black napkin, the bartender who told me he even spent his days off there, to the manager who described the place as "one big house." I could tell our waitress Jenn, genuinely enjoyed her job and was very knowledgeable about the menu.

Some Kinda Good is all about good food and good company, and when the two are combined, that's a life well lived. The Optimist is a breath of fresh air for the city life, a nautical escape. My friend Harper said it perfectly, "That wasn't just going out to dinner–that was the best two-hour dining experience of my life."

Dining the Way the South Intended

South City Kitchen
June 25, 2012

In a city as large as Atlanta, Georgia choosing a place to dine is like being on a weight-loss plan and trying to fill your plate with only your favorite dishes on Thanksgiving. That was the situation last Saturday as we drove around the A-T-L in search of the perfect brunch spot. It was South City Kitchen that won me over–the lively patio full of happy customers drew me in and as soon as I laid eyes on the menu, I knew we'd made the right choice.

We were greeted politely, then led through the cool, sophisticated dining room out onto the more relaxed patio. We took a seat in the wicker chairs and soon after, our well-dressed waiter delivered a bread basket and poured us up a cold glass of purified water. It's the little details that really take a dining experience up a notch, like watching your server pour water into a clean drinking glass while sitting outside in the June humidity.

Filled with warm, soft biscuits and golden corn muffins, the basket also sported softened butter and cold apple butter for spreading. One bite of that biscuit and it was circa 1991 and I was in my Grandma's kitchen without a care in the world.

On the menu, you'll find many southern classics like Buttermilk Fried Chicken, BBQ Pork Sandwiches, She-Crab Soup and Grits & Grillades. Unpredictable side options like corn and tomato, kale salad and fingerlings are a nice surprise. The prices ranged

anywhere from $5.95 for their House Made Granola to $19 for the Shrimp & Red Mule Grits- stone ground from Athens, Georgia.

The atmosphere is settling like a slower pace from a previous time. As a customer, you get the feeling you're a respected guest. The restaurant's most popular menu item is the Buttermilk Fried Chicken. Shrimp & Red Mule Grits takes second place.

I decided on the Buttermilk Fried Chicken and Waffle with pure maple syrup. I must admit, I've always been curious of the combination. Crazy as it seems, it works. The crunchy fried chicken with the buttery waffle...now I know why it's a Snoop Dogg favorite. Right on Snoop Doggy Dog!

We finished the meal with a sweet and fruity Watermelon Sorbet, available by one scoop or two, with coffee. Finding parking was the only challenge to eating here, but after the chicken & waffle dish, it sure didn't hurt me to walk a few blocks. Open since 1993, South City Kitchen lives up to its motto: Dining the Way the South Intended.

SAVANNAH

A Saturday Morning Tradition

Back in the Day Bakery
June 17, 2012

At the intersection of West 40th and Bull Streets under one lone palm tree in the Starland District of Savannah, Georgia sits Back in the Day Bakery, so fondly known as *The Best Little Bakery in the South*. I had wanted to visit for weeks, ever since I'd seen Cheryl Day, co-owner, cooking with Paula Deen on Food Network.

It was everything I'd hoped it would be and more. I was in love from the moment I entered. Love at first sight. It was like sensory overload. The smell of fresh bread. The cottage, rustic, modern style. The retro appliances. The vintage dishes. The coastal color palette. The inviting seating area immediately caught my eye–I couldn't get over the live baby's breath anchored in tin pails and the oversized chairs. This was a place I could come daily, I thought.

Rosemary Ciabatta bread and Pugliese loaves (a crusty Italian bread), along with Sunny Lemon Bars and Bourbon Bread Pudding fill the window as you approach the cashier to place your order. Then I saw it. Cinnamon Sticky Buns. It just so happened that I had visited Back in the Day bakery on a special day–Saturday morning, the only time of the week Griff Day, co-owner, bakes these unbelievably freakin' good send-you-to-church delicacies. Made with local honey from the Savannah Bee Company, the buns have a sweet-spicy filling, a caramel

glaze and a tangy, oh-my-sweet-heavenly-Lord, cream cheese frosting. The taste was enough to make this Southern Baptist begin speaking in tongues.

I enjoyed my Cinnamon Sticky Bun with a cup of the Bakery's best-selling organic breakfast tea. The floor and countertops are cement, just another little detail that adds to the nostalgia. Simple syrup, a combination of equal parts water and sugar, is available to sweeten your tea or coffee. I like using simple syrup because it allows you to be in control of your sugar intake, of pristine importance when you're downing Cinnamon Sticky Buns.

You'll also find utensils for the taking in classic Mason Jars. Back in the Day Bakery doesn't just sell baked goods – lunch is also served daily from 11 a.m. – 4 p.m. I ordered the Rosemary Chicken sandwich, made with chicken, red onion, celery, black currants and herb spiced mayo. The Days have really succeeded in creating a true experience.

The food draws you in and the atmosphere makes you want to stay. The Bakery opened in 2002. Their best seller? An Old-Fashioned Vanilla Cupcake with Vanilla Buttercream. The cupcakes were fresh from the oven. Even the staff members are colorful. Decked out in aprons with handkerchiefs on their heads, they offer friendly service with a smile. My trip wouldn't have been complete without purchasing The Back in the Day Bakery Cookbook. Buy it from the Bakery and you'll get an autographed copy! If the recipes contained in this book taste anything like the Saturday-morning tradition Cinnamon Sticky Buns, it'll be the best $24.95 I've ever spent.

An Old School Savannah Experience, The Crystal Beer Parlor Delivers

June 25, 2013

At the intersection of Jefferson and West Jones streets located just a few blocks away from the Savannah Civic Center, *The Crystal Beer Parlor* has immediate mystique. The name alone conjures up curiosity, and upon stepping through the front door, you know you've arrived somewhere special. The ambiance is enough to peak your interest but wait until you taste the food.

Framed black and white photographs fill the hallways, dining rooms and the historic bar area of the once family-grocer-turned-restaurant, depicting Savannah's past and images of Tybee Island, timeworn race cars and famous guests. Daily specials are presented on a chalkboard near the hostess stand. A pay phone hangs on the wall as memorabilia, reminding patrons of days gone by.

Dressed in all black, the servers wear white pinstriped aprons. Our waiter Greg, a native Savannahian, answered every question we had, providing his favorite menu recommendations, when asked to choose between the options we'd narrowed down. Prices range from $3.25 for a classic Caesar side salad to $23.95 for a seafood combo plate. Straight forward and knowledgeable regarding the food and the restaurant, Greg was filled with fun facts about The Crystal Beer Parlor you'd never know unless you asked.

Greg recalled his Grandmother's perception of the restaurant's speakeasy reputation in the 1930s with a laugh. "I can

remember my Grandma talking about The Crystal Beer Parlor like it was the Devil's playground back then. She'd roll over in her grave if she knew I was working here." Savannah's second oldest restaurant, The Crystal Beer Parlor was one of the first American restaurants to serve alcohol after the repeal of prohibition.

To start, we ordered the down home Gawgia Cracka Nachos. With a name like that, it was too hard to pass up. Featuring barbecued, smoked, pulled pork piled high on crispy tortilla chips and topped with cheddar cheese, diced raw onion, jalapenos and chopped dill pickles, it was like a barbecue sandwich deconstructed. In the words of my boyfriend Kurt, a local, "I'm here to tell you, that's some good eatin'."

Known for their burgers, hand-cut French fries and crab stew, the most popular item they serve is The Famous Crystal Burger, featuring a half pound of griddled ground chuck with all the condiments. It was moist and meaty with pure beef flavor. We also tried the fried shrimp sandwich toasted to perfection and served on a soft hoagie roll. Alongside it, the crispy sweet potato fries were the best I've tasted–anywhere. Their secret? Deep fry them frozen. There was no room left for dessert, but I can hardly wait to get back to try the Gawgia Peach Cobbler.

We ended our dining experience at the lively bar with a Tom Collins cocktail and a Palm beer, a Belgian ale with a clean finish. Since 1933, the bartenders have poured up what the restaurant's website deems the "Beers of Our Fathers." Offering a dozen American brews, Happy Hour is Monday – Friday from 4 – 7 p.m.

If old school Savannah is what you seek, visit The Crystal Beer Parlor. Complete with familiar food you'll know and love, staff members who exemplify Southern hospitality and an atmosphere that takes you back, you don't want to miss this Hostess City experience.

Let's Do Lunch: My Top 5 Savannah Mid-Day Meal Spots

July 29, 2017

I moved to Savannah, Georgia just before Christmas last year, and began a new full-time job in March. When you work from 8 a.m. to 5 p.m., the lunch hour is always a bright spot during the day.

It's nice to step away from the office for a change of scenery and to recharge for the afternoon, and while sometimes lunch is a sandwich at home or a quick drive-thru run, I revel in the days when I visit a quaint eatery, read over an enticing menu and anticipate my selection as I sip on a cold, refreshing dose of caffeine.

What makes a great lunch spot? Well, to me it's a mix of things, beginning with seasonal, local ingredients presented thought-fully, in a clean, inviting atmosphere with friendly people. Obviously, great flavor is a huge factor, good portion size and knowledgeable staff too. An informed server–someone who takes pride in their work and knowing the menu–gains imme-diate respect in my book.

My family and friends are always asking about where to eat in Savannah, and lately, I've been on a lunchtime quest to find the very best spots to share with you.

Here are my Top 5 Mid-Day Meal Spots in the Hostess City:

1   Kayak Kafe – Midtown

Hands down, Kayak Kafe has the menu to beat. From hearty salads to flavorful tacos and quesadillas, most ingredients are sourced locally and they're all natural. The Southwestern Wild Georgia Shrimp Tacos are packed with fresh ingredients, and creamy avocado right on top! What's not to love? I never visit Kayak Cafe without ordering a basket of their cinnamon-sugar laden sweet potato fries. They have great cocktails too, and even offer weekend brunch. With locations in both Midtown and Downtown Savannah, this is a must visit.

2   Joe's Homemade Cafe, Catering and Bakery

Joe's Homemade Cafe, Catering and Bakery is a hidden gem. Quaint but bursting with Southern hospitality, the inside of the restaurant has a handful of tables and each one is decked out with white table cloths and fresh flowers. The menu offers house-made desserts and pastries, plus sandwiches, salads and custom cakes. The lemon cheesecake is highly recommended.

Tomato Basil Soup & Chicken Panini with fresh fruit at Joe's Homemade Cafe

3 Chicken Salad Chick

It's a rare occasion when I give a restaurant chain any play. BUT Chicken Salad Chick is the exception. Founded by Stacey Brown, a stay-at-home mom from Alabama with help from her computer software salesman-husband, this franchise offers 15 different flavors of chicken salad! It is the first restaurant I have ever been to that has grape salad as a side option. How phenomenal! Grape salad is a special treat I only ever make at home and they do it just right with brown sugar and pecans. I could go on and on about the menu, the brand and the atmosphere. My favorite menu item is ironically, not chicken salad at all, but the Pimento Cheese BLT. I order mine spicy, always with a side of grape salad. Every plate is served with a sweet treat to finish the meal – a buttercream frosted flower cookie that literally melts in your mouth. The signage will make you laugh out loud – especially in the ladies' room. Southerners, don't miss this fine establishment.

4 Sandfly BBQ

I couldn't possibly write a post about good lunches in the South without including at least one BBQ joint. Sandfly BBQ is an award-winning restaurant in a small community in Savannah. My office is close by, and whenever I'm craving smoked barbecue, this place hits the spot. With hand-cut French fries and a variety of sauces, their meat is traditionally seasoned and smoked over a combination of hickory and pecan wood. It's a walk-up-and-order-at-the-counter kind of joint, with a few booths on the inside and outdoor seating. I order the BBQ pulled pork sandwich with fries, take a book along and sip on sweet tea.

5 SoHo South Cafe

If you love an eclectic atmosphere and a good Southern menu, look no further than the elegant SoHo South. With offerings like fried okra, Georgia peach salad, chicken and waffles, braised collard greens and buttermilk biscuits, you'll feel right at home. Lunch is often accompanied by live piano music, creating a bustling yet peaceful ambiance. I love the Fried Green Tomato Sandwich with toasted goat cheese and sweet tomato-oregano jam, with a side of sweet potatoes. The fish tacos with corn salsa and avocado are also noteworthy. One of Savannah's staple lunch and Sunday Brunch spots, the restaurant morphs into an event venue easily, and gets its inspiration and namesake from a New York City neighborhood.

Forsyth Farmers' Market: A Food Lover's Paradise

April 15, 2013

There's something so personable about shopping at a farmers' market. Where else can you get one-on-one information from the farmer himself about an uncommon fruit, or learn about the flavor and richness of free-range eggs? At a grocery store, the produce department employee may be able to tell you what's out-of-stock and when the next shipment comes in, but the likelihood of discovering their favorite way to prepare radishes or the secret to pairing fresh herbs with complimentary dishes will probably not come up in conversation. I don't know of many places where you can conveniently talk directly to the beekeeper about the differences in local honey varieties or learn how long it takes made-from-scratch bread to rise directly from

the hands of the baker. It's a food lover's paradise–and it's benefits like these that get me out of bed on Saturday morning to visit the Forsyth Farmers' Market.

Every Saturday from 9 a.m. to 1 p.m. at the South end of Forsyth Park in the majestic city of Savannah, area farmers and volunteers set up their tables and tents and prop up their sidewalk chalkboards advertising the week's just-picked seasonal produce, jellies and jams, prepared casseroles and various meats on refrigerated trucks like grass-fed ground beef, ribeye steak, pancetta and pork tenderloin. There's even homemade popsicles and locally roasted coffee. It's a casual, unpretentious environment where goods are wrapped in brown paper sacks and plastic bags, and prices are taped to baskets and labeled with a black marker.

You'll find whatever is in season. On my April visit, strawberries, red radishes, salad greens, sweet potatoes, scallions, snap peas and huge bundles of bright orange carrots were available. With a high of 84 degrees and clear blue skies, I strolled along the sidewalk under the Spanish-moss covered oak trees and decided on some beautiful sweet potatoes from South Carolina's Gruber Farm. I also picked up some small and large carrot bundles— yellow, purple and orange in color—from Walker Farms, along with wildflower honey from Register Georgia's B&G Honey Farm and fresh herbs from Ogeechee River Gardens. Each of the vendors were friendly and happy to carry on conversation.

Being a food blogger and an at-home cook, I welcome the challenge of cooking what's available. I like to think it sharpens my kitchen skill. I managed to use all my ingredients and came up with a hands-off side dish that's good for you and pretty on a plate. With a roasted, slightly sweet flavor, my Wildflower Honey Roasted Sweet Potatoes and Carrots with Dill & Thyme will have you throwing on your sunglasses and heading to the farmers' market faster than you can say E-I-E-I-O.

Wildflower Honey Roasted Sweet Potatoes and Carrots with Dill & Thyme

SERVES 2

- 1 large, peeled sweet potato cut into thin strips
- 1 small bundle of baby carrots cut lengthwise
- 2 regular size orange carrots cut lengthwise
- 2-3 tbsps of extra virgin olive oil
- Kosher salt
- Freshly ground black pepper
- 2 tbsps or more according to taste of wildflower honey
- Fresh dill & thyme, chopped

Preheat oven to 425 degrees. Place vegetables in a single layer on a baking sheet. Season with salt and pepper. Drizzle with olive oil and honey. Using your hands (a cook's best tools!), toss the vegetables to coat. Cook for 25 – 30 minutes. Place in a serving dish and top with chopped dill and sprigs of thyme. Drizzle with more honey if desired.

TYBEE ISLAND

Sophisticated Flavor in a Laid Back Kinda Style

Coco's Sunset Grille
January 28, 2014

During Tybee Island Restaurant Week, I had the privilege of meeting a fellow blogger–one of my longtime blog followers, and discovering a new place I had seen in the distance many times while crossing over the Lazaretto Creek Bridge, but had never taken the time to stop and explore. After a little menu research on participating restaurants, the Fried Strawberries at Coco's Sunset Grille caught my eye and the marina filled with shrimp boats and sunset views lured me in.

Immediately, Coco's has the feel of a fun and festive Florida vibe with its bright, cheerful paint colors and lively bar. While my boyfriend, Kurt and I were waiting to meet our friends, Jon and Lydia, we took a walk around the docks and saw the Bait & Tackle Shop and Kayak Rentals on the marina.

Our waitress, Megan, a laid back girl in holey jeans and a Hawaiian shirt, had a great sense of humor and made sure we were always taken care of.

We kicked things off with a couple of Landshark Lagers and dove right in to making our selections. For just $25, the special menu offered choices in appetizer, dinner and dessert categories. In the appetizer round, we had our choice of French Onion Soup, a Shrimp Cake, Fried Green Tomatoes or Bacon-Wrapped Scallops.

Served with a Thai-chili sauce, the scallops were presented atop a bed of greens alongside an inviting wedge of lemon. From the plating to the service, Coco's had me happy at every turn.

For my main course, I ordered the Shrimp Cakes with sautéed vegetables and mashed potatoes. This was something new for me. I had eaten crab cakes before, but never a shrimp cake. Cooked to perfection, the plump, wild Georgia shrimp were sweet within the seasoned breading and left me wanting more. Rustic including the red skins, the mashed potatoes sang on the plate. The house-made remoulade was mayonnaise based and one waitress commented, "I put it on everything. I even dip my fries in it."

Other dinner selections included Sirloin Steak Marsala with scalloped potatoes and grilled asparagus, and Thai Tuna with

wasabi mashed potatoes and sautéed veggies. Coco's is the place to go for sophisticated flavors minus the fuss of fine dining.

The Fried Strawberries totally surpassed my expectations! After the delicious meal we'd eaten, this came as no surprise. Served with fresh, sweetened whipped cream and a pretty pink strawberry sauce, the fresh fruit was fried in pancake batter and rolled in cinnamon sugar. I can't wait to recreate this experience at home. They were *Some Kinda Good!*

So much of a customer's dining experience is affected by a restaurant's environment. From the attitude of the staff to the sound of live entertainment and the tastefully decorated, clean bathrooms, Coco's Sunset Grille is a place I will definitely return, especially in the summertime. Their website took the words right out of my mouth–" Just add an ice-cold beer, great music and a few of your best friends, and you've got a recipe for Tybee living the way it's meant to be."

Where Friendship and Fine Food Collide

The Crab Shack
October 8, 2012

I'm convinced that all I really need in this world is a lifelong friend and a pile of crab legs on the Southern seacoast. There are times when my soul feels so content, like if in that moment life were to end, I could slip from the Earth with a smile on my face. That satisfaction, that fulfillment only comes from good conversation–the kind where you can bear your soul and not be judged, paired with the taste of food so fresh it was swimming in the Atlantic only moments before it landed on your plate. My blog, *Some Kinda Good* is all about good food and good company, and that's what I experienced over the weekend at The Crab Shack on Tybee Island with Jennifer, my friend of 17 years.

Located just off highway 80 as you make your way onto Tybee Island, The Crab Shack–Where the Elite Eat in Their Bare Feet–is *THE* destination for all things seafood. Known for their Lowcountry boil, the restaurant has been voted *Best Seafood* and *Best Outdoor Dining* since 1998.

Offering indoor and outdoor dining, there's really no bad seat in the house. When we first arrived, we sat on the deck overlooking Chimney Creek, and later moved inside to the screened in porch area when it started to rain. Since we visited in October, the boat was decorated for Halloween. From your table, you can hear boat motors cranking up and seagulls overhead.

The *menu* features the Captain Crab's Sampler where you can try an assortment of seasonal shellfish with corn, potatoes and sausage. It also offers a variety of crabs–Snow, Alaskan King, Blue, Dungeness or Stone. Not only does The Crab Shack serve seafood, but true to its Southern region, they tout "The best barbecue on the beach or anywhere else." The sides include corn, potatoes, sausage, smashed taters and slaw.

I ordered a Landshark Lager–only fitting being on the island–with a cup of Boston Clam Chowder and the Half and Half dinner: A half-pound of snow crab legs with a half-pound of wild Georgia shrimp. It came with corn on the cob. There are holes in the center of each table for discarding shrimp hulls and empty shells and I love being able to just toss your paper plate when you're done. It's casual dining on the coast, the way it should be.

A large deck overlooks the creek. Age old Spanish-moss covered oak trees hang over the area, creating an ambiance where it's impossible to be unhappy.

I counted 53 pelicans fishing over the ocean that evening, watched the sunset by the lighthouse and touched down in the Atlantic one more time. We rode 80 West back home with the windows down and Southern rock on the radio, the palm trees passing in the wind.

A Heavenly Vibe at Huc-A-Poo's

Huc-A-Poo's Bites & Booze
November 4, 2012

Huc-A-Poo's Bites & Booze is the epitome of life. It's where stories are born. It's the kind of place Pat Conroy and Ernest Hemingway write about in novels. It's a genuine, local bar with an environment that can't be created. It's not store-bought. It's not forced. No one has a care in the world. It's a place where nothing matters–what you wear, who you are, where you come from. You can just be. It's care free, non-judgmental. It's come one, come all. It's family owned and operated. It's the kind of place where time and seasons escape. Laid back. Eclectic. It doesn't have a website. You won't find brochures on it. It's not touristy. It's unpretentious, unassuming. The slogan on the paper menu reads: Huc-A-Poo's – *Where the Mind and Spirits Meet.* I would imagine heaven to have the same vibe.

The Cast of Characters

The people in a place make all the difference. It's the characters who create the atmosphere. Let me introduce you to the cast of characters who inspired my experience:

Steven

He wore a multi-colored Beanie hat and liked to call me brat, but oddly, in an endearing way. He said, "My brother owns this place. Want to meet him?" He led me into the kitchen, and I got a behind the scenes tour. Throughout the night, he would look at me across the room and put his finger to his lips and say, "shhhhh." He wandered from table to bar top to staircase and his brothers referred to him as Huc-A-Poo's PR guy. He was right at home.

The Bartender

He would pop out from behind the bar and groove to the music, moving from customer to customer bringing drinks, taking checks. He had a beard and obviously loved his job.

The Band

The Royal Noise: Jazz, Funk, Soul – Each band member bled music. It ran through their veins. They felt every note. They expressed pure passion in a saxophone, a drum set, a bass and electric guitar. It was evident they were born to play.

The Staff

A close knit group of folks who appeared to be all related. They were long-haired, free-spirited and kind with tanned skin worn from the sun. Very welcoming. Really hospitable. No uniforms, they wore whatever they pleased. Shorts, T-shirts, flip-flops, even in November.

The Food

Pizza. Beer. Saturday night. We ordered a $15 specialty pizza – The Federale: Mexican pizza with grilled chicken, red onions, bell

peppers, fresh tomatoes and jalapenos. It was massive and only $15 bucks. We'll get at least four meals out of it from the leftovers! Landshark Lagers with lime slices only made sense to drink.

You can order pizza by the $4 slice or a whole pie. Make your choice from 12 different specialty pies or build your own. Wraps, nachos and hot dogs are on the menu too, even low carb salads. The food tasted great, but honestly it wouldn't have mattered.

The Cost

Nothing on the menu is priced over $7 with the exception of the $15 whole pies, which would cost at least $30 anywhere else. Amazingly affordable.

The Location

The restaurant is located in the Tybee Oaks Shopping Center just a few miles from the beach off of Highway 80.

The Crowd

On a Saturday night in early November, the age group ranged from 25 – 60 with the majority of the crowd being locals, others, first-time visitors like myself.

Huc-A-Poo's combined all my favorite things in one place-Good food and good company, and live music in an incredible atmosphere on the Georgia coast. It's the kind of environment you happen upon once in a blue moon, the kind of place that has the potential to make me relocate. Huc-A-Poo's is a place that sets the standard, that you'll continue comparing other environments to again and again. They've found a new regular in me.

White Zinfandel and Wild Georgia Shrimp

Sting Ray's Seafood Restaurant
May 7, 2012

It's the kind of place you drive by and think, "We have to go there!" Maybe it's the sound of live beach music that lures you in or the colorful umbrellas and white lights. For me, it was the idea of strolling over from the beach, sun-kissed and sandy to enjoy some wild Georgia shrimp on the patio in the ocean breeze.

Around 7 p.m. on a Saturday night following a great day at the beach, we joined the crowd at Sting Ray's Seafood Restaurant located just across the street from the Atlantic ocean.

Wearing a little powder and lip gloss, dressed in my swimsuit cover-up and sparkling flip-flops, I ordered a cold glass of white zinfandel and enjoyed the music. The casual, laid-back atmosphere is such a nice change of pace from the everyday office environment.

The menu was full of good food and it was hard to make a choice. You can order seafood by itself *or* as a meal, which is great if you don't have a huge appetite. I ordered a 1/2 pound of steamed, peel & eat wild Georgia shrimp with a house salad. Nothing fancy here-just simple, familiar ingredients with a cold drink. They were the most plump, succulent shrimp I've ever eaten. Served with melted butter and seasoned with Old Bay, the shrimp were swimming in the Atlantic just two days before they were served to me. Fresh at its finest. I squeezed the lemon juice right over the top and dunked them in cocktail sauce.

While we ate, live music entertained everyone well with classic beach tunes like Sittin' on the Dock of the Bay and It's 5 O'Clock Somewhere. Sting Ray's sits at the intersection of Butler Avenue and 14th Street. Every table was full, but the wait wasn't long. Who's counting minutes anyway when you're on island time?

After dinner, we took a walk on the pier to listen to the waves crash and say goodbye to the Atlantic one more time. It really wasn't goodbye though, only see you later–because I'll be back soon, and very soon.

ST. SIMONS ISLAND

Dine Southern Style on the Georgia Coast with Barbara Jean

Barbara Jean's Restaurant & Bar
December 10, 2012

There's something comforting about the never changing–those restaurants you've been going to for years that you know and love and have come to expect. You know the quality; you would bet your life savings by the she crab soup and nothing excites you more than sharing the experience with friends and family who've never tasted and seen. At the corner of Mallory and Beachview streets located in the Pier Village of St. Simons Island, Georgia sits one of my family's constants: Barbara Jean's. You may have visited in the Golden Isles, or in one of the four locations in South Carolina or Florida. Whether you go for the famous crab cakes or the pumpkin bread and the sweet jalapeno cornbread with cinnamon butter, Barbara Jean's *Easy Southern Dining* makes deciding where to eat lunch or dinner a cinch!

My favorite seat in the house is by the bay window overlooking the Pier Village shops. In the summertime, every table is usually full, and the place is bustling with wait staff, busboys and hungry tourists and locals. Traveling with Fido? Grab a seat on the patio. Dining alone? Pull up a chair at the full bar and order up your favorite cocktail. The *menu* prices range from $4.99 for a cup of soup to about $24 for the most expensive dinner entrée.

The food is *Some Kinda Good* y'all, and my best friend swears by "The Chocolate Stuff." Cobbler-like and better than a brownie, it's Barbara Jean's signature dessert and is served in a big bowl with homemade whipped cream. Other menu items include Tuna Steaks, Shrimp & Grits and Chicken Fried Steak. The restaurant is coastal and down home all at the same time—my kinda place!

After dinner, walk along Mallory street or take a seat at the Pier to see what the fisherman are reeling in. Of all the places to eat in the Golden Isles, Barbara Jean's should be at the top of your list.

Passion Meets Barbeque in Coastal Southeast Georgia

Southern Soul Barbeque
September 2, 2012

In the South, barbeque is a holy subject. Opinions about it begin forming at a very early age. At an after-church dinner recently, my sister-in-law and I were serving our plates and chatting about how good the barbeque looked, when a young boy not more than ten spoke up, confidence in motion, to let us know that while lunch was nice, it was his dad who made the *best* barbeque in all of Bulloch County. We take our pork seriously. Harrison and the staff at Southern Soul Barbeque on St. Simons Island get that. It's an expression from their very soul, spoken in tender pork, slow cooked and oak-smoked for hours over burning coals and served to anyone with sense enough to stop. You can see the smoke and smell that barbeque coming from the outdoor pits as soon as you hit the parking lot.

Harrison Sapp is co-owner. He was an all-around nice guy and made me and my Shih Tzu, Ewok, feel as welcome as a whelk in its shell. This guy gets up at 4 a.m. every day and begins cooking at 6:30 a.m. to have lunch ready for all the hungry folks in the Golden Isles. Passion is the only thing that would motivate one to do something so well seven days a week. He showed me around and lifted the lid on the smoker to reveal racks of beautiful pork butts cooking over hot coals lined up three deep. Seasoned with a sweet dry rub and sprayed with a little apple juice throughout the cooking process, the result is pure pork flavor, juicy and tender.

200

Ewok made himself right at home on the cool cement floor outside while I waited for my sandwich. The staff even brought him a bowl of water to drink. The long picnic tables are situated on the porch under a vaulted ceiling with big fans and drop lighting. It's the kind of casual atmosphere where it's perfectly acceptable to stroll over off the beach in your swimsuit. Served on a toasted bun with pickles, the Jumbo Pulled Pork Sandwich is a beautiful display of the restaurant's finest. I ordered creamy mac & cheese as my side with a tall, cold glass of sweet tea. Suffice it to say, it's the best $6.50 I've ever spent. Is your mouth watering yet? I drizzled my sandwich with a little Sweet Georgia Soul Sauce and dug in. Jars of sweet and hot sauce, vinegar and Texas Pete grace the tables. If slaw suits your fancy, they'll top your sandwich with it at no charge.

Formerly a 1940's gas station, tag plates and catchy signs decorate the restaurant front and posters advertising local events

fill the windows, giving the place that hometown, log cabin-like feel. I particularly love the Dig on Pig sign. On the menu, you'll find grilled pimento cheese sandwiches, beef brisket, chicken strips, ribs, even sausage and burgers. The sides are soulful too including selections like Brunswick stew, hoppin' john, fried okra and fried green beans.

No worries for all of you that prefer to beat the heat. Pull up a bar stool inside in the air conditioning and have a cold one. Southern Soul Barbeque is open Monday – Saturday from 11 a.m. - 10 p.m. and Sunday from 11 a.m. – 4 p.m. For a taste of Southern Soul at home, pick up a bottle of one of their Georgia Soul sauces.

As seen in leading magazines like *Georgia Trend, Garden & Gun* and *Southern Living* and on major television networks like *TLC* and *Food Network*, Southern Soul Barbeque is no secret. Guy Fieri himself has been here and has featured the restaurant on his show, *Diners, Drive-Ins and Dives*. This Southeast coastal Georgia smoke joint gets around. Located on the roundabout at 2020 Demere Road, be sure to pull in on your next visit to the Golden Isles of Georgia. It's worth the stop and good for your soul.

Start the Day at Palmer's Village Cafe

Palmer's Village Cafe
July 15, 2012

Breakfast on vacation. It's probably my favorite meal. Whether you rise with the sun or sleep until 10 a.m., the food at Palmer's Village Cafe on St. Simons Island will motivate you to get up and moving. They take pride in their ingredients and present plates with no detail undone. I've never been when there isn't a crowd and that's because, where there's good food, you'll find people.

I appreciate the thoughtfulness of the menu items. There aren't many places you can go to find an omelet with crab meat and homemade pimento cheese garnished with grilled, pickled okra. The dishes are regional too, like the Coastal Delight: an open-faced whole egg omelet topped with goat cheese, sautéed shrimp, spiced pecans and arugula. Smack dab between the Island hardware store and a small real estate company on Mallery Street, locals and vacationers fill the seats at Palmer's. It's my favorite place to start the day on the Island.

I ordered the Challah Bread French Toast served with Palmer's Village Cafe signature maple syrup. You won't find store bought syrup here. The Fresh Fruit side dish had juicy orange segments, sliced bananas and red strawberries. Now, y'all didn't think I forgot the meat, did you? Not just bacon or sausage...country ham. Salty and seasoned just right. That's what I'm talkin' 'bout! Artwork by local artists decorates the walls and is available for purchase. Open for breakfast and lunch, you'll feel welcome from the moment you step inside the creaking front door. No matter how busy Palmer's may be, the staff members will make sure your coffee cup is full and you've always got everything you need.

Best Breakfast Buffet in Town

Sandcastle Cafe & Grill
May 31, 2012

It was a sunny Saturday morning and 81 degrees when I strolled over to Sandcastle Cafe & Grill for breakfast in the St. Simons Island Village. By 9 a.m., many islanders and tourists had beat me there, already seated reading The Brunswick News, sipping on piping hot cups of coffee. I made my way through the crowd and happily opted for indoor seating in the A.C.

The cafe opened in 1989 and has since fed many a hungry tourist and locals alike. With exposed brick throughout and an eclectic mix of decorations, the atmosphere is casual and the food comforting. For an affordable price, you'll get the "Glorious Breakfast Buffet" including just about any breakfast food you can conjure up. You'll also receive unlimited pancakes, French toast and waffles. Or, feel free to order from the menu, where you can test your ticker with their signature Eggs Aorta-biscuits topped with gravy, scrambled eggs, sausage and cheddar cheese. Saving room for lunch? Try the lighter fare–the Fruit Plate with fresh seasonal fruit and homemade muffins.

I got the breakfast buffet so I could pick and choose a few of my favorites–hash browns, fresh fruit, grits and sausage. The coffee mug was just the right size. Guests help themselves to the wide array of buffet options. Sandcastle Cafe & Grill is open for breakfast, lunch and dinner. I don't know of any other place on the island where you'll get more for your money.

The fresh, cold fruit and orange juice are a welcomed relief from the summer sun. Black and white images fill the long brick wall. Framed by the owner herself some 20 years ago, the pictures depict St. Simons Island in the 1950's and local families whose descendants still eat at Sandcastle Cafe & Grill today.

Located at the end of the strip mall in the St. Simons Island Village, the cafe faces the recently renovated Neptune Park and is just steps away from my favorite island spot, the Pier.

STATESBORO

Gnat's Landing

When a single place comes to mind for lunch, going out on a Friday night *and* entertaining company, it's a winner. That's Gnat's Landing of Statesboro. The versatile bar & grill is family friendly and college town worthy. It's a natural choice for lunch before a Saturday afternoon football game in the Eagle Nation, or place to catch a good band and go out dancing on a Friday night. It's that hometown joint you can hardly visit without running into

someone you know. Christmas lights year 'round. Live music every weekend. Beer can and chicken wire decorum. What's not to love? The local favorite boasts a wide selection of American food with a Southern, coastal vibe in a casual and bright atmosphere.

Gnat's is my all-time favorite spot for lunch in the 'Boro. My friends and I call it "Ol' faithful." I have two lunchtime standbys at Gnat's and they never fail me: 1) Shrimp & Grits and 2) the Crab Cake Sandwich with Sweet Potato Fries. The food is always on point. The Shrimp & Grits is served with andouille sausage and bacon surrounded by toasted bread. Seasoned just right, it's warm, comforting and takes me to the coast. Served with cocktail sauce, the Crab Cake Sandwich features a large crab cake that's seared to perfection and served on toasted bread with tomato and lettuce. On occasion, I branch out and try something new like the BBQ Sandwich or the Blackened Chicken Caesar Salad. The menu also offers wraps, a great grilled chicken sandwich and unexpected side options like grits. I enjoy the Chef's attention to detail and presentation. They always sprinkle the rim of each dish with Parmesan cheese and fresh herbs.

Open more than seven years, Gnat's Landing of Statesboro is one of only two locations in Georgia. I've also visited the St. Simons Island restaurant in Red Fern Village. Though the weather is rarely cold enough to use it, Gnat's dining room in Statesboro even has a fireplace which creates a wonderful ambiance in the winter. Located on South Main Street in the heart of town, the restaurant also offers ample parking. Depending on when you go, the environment at Gnat's is bustling. Visit for Trivia on Tuesday nights, Karaoke on Wednesdays and Happy Hour all day on Sunday and Monday. No matter the time of day, they'll always have affordable drinks, daily lunch specials and a football game on the big screen.

With a name like Gnat's Landing, this Statesboro front-runner is right at home in the "Gnat Capitol of America."

Lunch A Latte at The Daily Grind

November 20, 2013

The first place to cross your mind when deciding on a lunch locale may not be a coffee shop, but when you visit Statesboro's The Daily Grind, the Gingerbread Latte won't be the only thing that tempts you. Serving up more than freshly roasted espresso beans, I'm totally impressed by the plates they produce out of that tiny little kitchen, like Roasted Red Pepper Soup with Smoked Gouda, Hot Ham and Cheese Croissants, Shrimp and Roasted Corn Soup and an array of other nutrient-packed wraps, inventive salads and flavored teas. Open since 2000, the quaint and cozy hideaway boasts a notable Noonday menu, but wait until you discover the 14-layer cakes, giant cookies and homemade muffins.

On the day I ordered the Grilled Chicken Bacon Ranch wrap, I remember tweeting this photo with the words, "This is the kind of pretty little lunch that inspires me to write." Presentation is everything. At The Daily Grind, they take great care in plating. Whether it's an over-sized coffee mug brimming with fresh whipped cream and steaming hot mocha or a cup of soup, when your order is up, it's placed on a feminine and delicate doily and served alongside a single napkin-tucked utensil.

Cold beverages are served in faux, branded hurricane goblets. One guest commented, "I've never felt so elegant drinking Mountain Dew." It's these special touches and subtle notes of

detail that add to the comfortable home-away-from-home vibe. Customers have their choice of fountain drinks, sweet or unsweetened tea, and flavored teas including raspberry, pomegranate, peach, mango, kiwi and my personal favorite– blackberry. Arabic coffee beans like Pumpkin Pie and Caramel are also roasted in small batch orders.

The atmosphere sets *The Daily Grind* apart. Large area rugs cover the cement floors, two wingback chairs sit directly in front of the fireplace and a mixture of round and square tables fill the dining room. You can also take a seat at the bar area and read the morning news or catch up on your Facebook news feed. No matter where you chose to sit, it's easy to slip into a corner with a good book and enjoy a cup of Joe. A tip jar near the cash register reads, "Thanks a Latte." The menu features soups, sandwiches, wraps and sides like chips, pickles and cookies. Open Monday – Friday from 6:45 a.m. – 10 p.m., and Saturdays from 8 a.m. – 5 p.m., live music happens every Friday night. As a college student circa 2001, I was a regular at this unique spot. Twelve years later, that fact hasn't changed.

Ellis Farm Fresh Meats, The Hometown Grocer

February 6, 2014

Every dot on the map needs a hometown grocer–a personable place to load up your buggy with beef, to be called "darlin'" by the cashier at checkout, and where you know your butcher by name. They're the jewels of small towns, the businesses that give a city personality. Ellis Farm Fresh Meats has served Bulloch County for more than 40 years in that very capacity. "The Biggest Little Meat Market in Statesboro" began as a meat plant in 1968 in the Ellis family backyard of Hopeulikit (a small community between Statesboro and Portal). Local farmers

visited the family from miles around bringing livestock to be slaughtered and packaged for the freezer. "My dad wanted to start his own business so he and mother could stay close at home with my brothers and sisters," said Kimball Ellis, co-owner of Ellis Farm Fresh Meats. Twenty years later, the little store with a red tin roof sits on West Main Street in downtown Statesboro, in the former location of Maryland Fried Chicken. Ellis Farm Fresh Meats opened to the public in the early 1980s to meet the needs of a growing, changing community.

Today, the family-owned-and-operated business offers custom cut meats, seafood and a premium line of frozen vegetables, but it isn't necessarily the prime cuts of beef, or the low country boil pots that have roped me in. I've never visited the store before when I haven't seen shopping carts filled to the brim with those pink packages of center cut pork chops and fresh ground chuck hamburger meat wrapped in cellophane, or when there hasn't been a line surrounding the squared off cash registers at the entrance of the store. The atmosphere is nothing fancy, and that's what it makes it one-of-a-kind. The vintage red and gray checkerboard flooring hints at days gone by, and the customers' casual chatter with one another makes an everyday shopping trip feel like homecoming. It's the kind of place you walk in and think, "Why have I not been here before?" and when you look around at all the folks shopping, you're wondering how they could keep such a treasure to themselves. Of the 26 employees, ten are family members. The other longtime workers, like butchers Jerry and Eric, have been with the owners for many years and are considered part of the Ellis family too. "You will see Eric and Jerry at the meat market every day. They are just two of our dedicated employees," said Ellis. Jerry has worked at the market for 12 years, helping to manage inventory and as a butcher. Eric has been with the company for 22 years.

Though the business is known for its meat selection, home-made sausages and gator tail aren't the only items flying off the shelves. Something you'll notice right off the bat when you visit the market is the support for other local farmers and vendors. You'll find products like Freeman's Mill Grits and B&G Honey for sale, along with Braswell Food Company's salad dressings and specialty sauces. Perhaps the most exciting item available for the baker in me, is the old fashioned 14-layer homemade cakes, sold by the halves, in uncommon flavors like key lime and strawberry. They even have peanut butter extract, and that's not something you see every day.

With Valentine's Day just around the bend, I asked Kimball to share a romantic recipe for two that customers could get from Ellis Farm Fresh Meats and prepare at home. He suggests picking up two choice rib eye steaks, two twice-baked potatoes and making a toss salad to serve with your favorite dressing. When it comes to having dinner with your sweetheart, Kimball says, "The best eatin' is at home."

JULIET

The Whistle Stop Cafe

November 3, 2014

"After Ruth died and the railroad stopped runnin', the cafe shut down and everybody just scattered to the winds. It was never more'n just a little knockabout place, but now that I look back on it, when that cafe closed, the heart of the town just stopped beatin'. It's funny how a little place like this brought so many people together."

—Ninny Threadgoode,
Fried Green Tomatoes

On a beautiful fall day recently, my mom and boyfriend, Kurt, ventured to have lunch at the Whistle Stop Cafe, made famous by the 1991 movie "Fried Green Tomatoes," a comedy-drama based on the novel Fried Green Tomatoes at the Whistle Stop Cafe by Fannie Flagg. Though the movie plot is set in 1920's Alabama, the filming took place in Juliette, Georgia. It's one of those films that every Southerner can relate to; every character in the movie is identifiable as one's own family member. The cafe was everything I'd imagined it would be: country with a wide front porch complete with rocking chairs and large ferns, inviting in a way that reminds you of a simpler time and place, and authentic with a menu that proclaims Southern culture and cultivates deep-seated food memories in the hearts and minds of every diner.

We drank sweet iced tea served in Mason jars with big wedges of lemon and bit into the crunchy, highly anticipated Fried Green Tomato appetizer to the tune of Hank Williams Jr.'s "Country State of Mind." The hand sliced green tomatoes were battered and fried to perfection, and you could see flecks of black pepper in the coating. Served with made-from-scratch radish sauce, it tasted much like a spicy Thousand Island dressing, though the waitress was tight-lipped with the recipe. We placed our orders — Country Fried Steak with mashed potatoes and gravy and Brunswick stew for Kurt, Yard Bird Tenders with collard greens, grilled squash and zucchini for mama, and the Fried Green Tomato Burger featuring Swiss cheese, lettuce, onion, bacon and radish sauce, with sweet potato fries for me. What I loved most about the menu was how the Fried Green Tomato was elevated — featured in an appetizer, a salad, a sandwich and on a burger, the restaurant's name is not in vain. Prices ranged around $9 an order to $22 for a full rack of Smoked Baby Back ribs.

For dessert, we split a slice of seven-layer lemon cheesecake with vanilla bean ice cream. The cake was moist and light, with tangy sheets of lemon filling between each layer. Other dessert options included peach cobbler, pecan cobbler, apple dumpling and chocolate bread pudding.

The once general merchandising store-turned-cafe still contains an antique file system loaded with old yellow tickets from the past along with the meat block, cash register, meat scales, wood heater, safe and other items used from 1927 to 1972. Movie memorabilia and local history also adorn the walls. Folks sit on bar stools at the u-shaped counter top in the center of the restaurant, or in tables and booths. The floors squeak and ceiling fans keep the air flowing.

The wait staff wear t-shirts that say, "Get Fried at the Whistle Stop Cafe," and bustle about welcoming tourists and locals.

If you've never seen the movie, watch it. If you've never read the book, read it. And if you've never eaten at the cafe, plan a trip. You'll be glad you did.

Good food and good company, that's what it's all about!

AUGUSTA

Rae's Coastal Cafe: An Inland Island Hideaway

June 13, 2014

Two of my best friends recently took me to dinner at a place more than 153 miles inland from the Georgia Coast located in my hometown of Augusta, Georgia. They promised it would be "right up my alley" and said I should "be prepared to blog about it." Though it's been open since I was nine years old, that Friday night was the first time I'd ever heard of it or set foot through its doors. Tucked away in a small community at the west end of Walton Way, Rae's Coastal Cafe transported me to the islands the moment I stepped inside, perpetuated only by the best Key Lime Pie Martini I've ever had, and a house salad that rivaled my go-to Caesar and sailed away with my heart.

The cafe touched on every indicator I consider noteworthy about a restaurant: 1) It's independently owned, 2) The local, casual atmosphere was well done–coastal but not in an obnoxious way, 3) The food was excellent and 4) The service was informed.

Our waitress was April. Servers can make or break a dining experience and if they're on point, nine times out of 10, your visit will be too. April was well-informed on the menu items, at the ready with refills, and intuitively aware of when to ask if we were ready for the next course or if she could take our empty plates. As a first-time visitor, she sold me on the house salad when I routinely ordered a Caesar, and I'm so glad I took her word. Super friendly and seemingly happy to be at work, April enhanced our meal and represented Rae's expertly well.

There on the table, much to my surprise sat a product from good ol' Statesboro...Braswell's Vidalia Onion Steak Sauce. That made this Statesboro food writer proud.

The meal began with fresh-baked rolls, served with spread-able butter, followed by Rae's Famous House Salad, known as an Augusta favorite. A simple combination of fresh greens and tomatoes tossed in a homemade dressing, the salad is plated in a cold, pewter-like bowl and topped with crunchy croutons made in-house. It was everything one could hope for–light, tangy, crunchy and refreshing.

I ordered the Blackened Mahi-Mahi, a healthy 9 oz. fillet topped with Cajun spices, seared in a cast iron skillet and served with new potatoes. April informed me that Rae's uses the same spices on the fish as in their famous Jamaican Jerk Chicken. The Mahi-Mahi had the perfect kick to it and together with the buttery potatoes, I was happy and satisfied. My friends shared the special that evening: Carolina Mountain Trout with crisp green beans and new potatoes. For dessert, we tackled a slice of Chocolate Cheesecake made with Kahlua and drizzled with raspberry syrup. Other tempting menu items included Coconut Fried Shrimp, the Crabmeat Sandwich (yes, that's right. Not crab cake, crabMEAT!), the Dolphin Sandwich and Filet Mignon. Chicken, steak, seafood...they do it all!

It's a good thing that I no longer live in Augusta because I would have to have this drink in my life every day. Rimmed in a graham cracker crust, the Key Lime Pie Martini was the most balanced blend of sweet and tart I've ever experienced. It was like drinking pie. Move over Malibu Bay Breeze, there's a new sheriff in town.

Dining at Rae's Coastal Cafe felt like an episode of Cheers. The owner, Walter, makes his way through the restaurant greeting guests and shaking hands. You're bound to run into someone you know there. It's a comfortable place where people go to enjoy good food and good company...after all, that's what it's all about!

NORTH AUGUSTA

Longtime North Augusta Restaurant Serves Up Seafood & Southern Hospitality

Old McDonald Fish Camp Seafood Restaurant
May 12, 2016

For those of us who grew up near Augusta, Georgia, a trip out to Old McDonald Fish Camp is always a treat. My family has enjoyed going for years–we pick up my Grandma on the way, and head out to the country for some grits and hushpuppies, hoping to get there before the waiting room fills up. We usually visit on a Friday or Saturday night, but recently, I realized we'd been doing it all wrong! Thursday night is Crab Leg Night and the only night of the week my favorite crustaceans make an appearance.

For a reasonable price, you get one and a half pounds of Canadian King Crab Legs, that's three clusters worth. I ordered mine with a baked potato. The aforementioned hushpuppy and grits bar are complimentary with every meal, along with little paper cups filled with coleslaw.

I have never been happier than the moment a thick piece of intact crab meat is released from its shell. Packets of butter are available at the self-serve, all-you-can-eat grits and hush-puppy bar, and tin pails containing salt & pepper, ketchup and everything you need sit atop the blue and white checkered tablecloths. Sweet tea is served in mason jars. Other menu items like boiled shrimp, Lowcountry Boil, Po' Boys and lots of fried seafood selections are always available. My grandma just LOVES the catfish! The restaurant offers wild game, including quail and gator too.

In true country fashion, the wait staff wear blue jean overalls and tie-dyed t-shirts. The restaurant is decorated with farm equipment and stuffed peacocks, open floor plan style, and surrounded by large picture windows providing all the diners with a pond view. What's better than eating a mound of succulent crab legs on the water? Outside, goats and baby goats, ducks and chickens roam around the fenced-in area. You can even feed the farm animals! I especially love the cats.

Family owned and operated since 1977, the restaurant began with an original seating capacity of 95 and now seats over 250. I love what owner Jay Bass says on the history of the place: "Old McDonald Fish Camp is truly a family business. My parents were the backbone. Daddy had the dream, and Mama had the recipes. The hushpuppies, tartar sauce, cocktail sauce, and iced tea were all created in our family kitchen."

This is a place you're sure to receive Southern hospitality, be fed well and entertained. Make it a weekend destination or a Thursday night on the town—whenever you choose to go, you'll be glad you did.

UVALDA

South Georgia Restaurant Offers River Views, Large Portions and Wild Game

Benton Lee's Steakhouse
March 7, 2016

There are steakhouses, and then there's Benton Lee's. I have discovered the place to eat meat in South Georgia, y'all. If you're looking for a good steak, stop your search right now and hop in your car for a drive through the country. Known for its large portions and family-centered atmosphere, the restaurant, with its wide front porch and back deck, overlooks the Altamaha River. For many reading this though, it won't be a surprise. The locals of this community have enjoyed Benton Lee's Steakhouse for 48 years.

My good lookin' husband, Kurt, and I drove over to the restaurant from Claxton, Georgia on a Friday night, just in time to catch the sunset.

We ordered gator nuggets to start, because that's what you do when you live in The Fruitcake Capital of the World and no restaurant within a 30-mile radius has it on the menu. Much to my dismay, the gator served at Benton Lee's is not wrestled and caught from the muddy waters of the Altamaha (ha!), but sourced from a gator farm in Odom, Georgia about 300 miles away. Gator has a tough and chewy consistency, but everyone should try it once. Our server said he liked it better than chicken, but I'll stick with poultry (spoken like a true resident of Evans County).

The straightforward menu features steaks of all cuts and sizes, plus seafood-shrimp, oysters and catfish–chicken tenders and wild game like quail, gator and frog legs. Staples including hamburger steak, pork chops and chef salad also are available. We ordered the Sirloin for Two: each serving is individually cooked and is at least 12 ounces. In the casual atmosphere, tea and water are self-serve.

The hand-cut fries are perfectly salted and crunchy. My steak was cooked to a medium temperature, juicy and just right. Tender and warm from the grill, the steak melts in your mouth. Beautiful grill marks make an appetizing presentation, and a standard salad and roll round out the meal. I am told that once upon a time Benton Lee's Steakhouse hosted a competition where if you ate six pounds worth of beef, you would get it for free. I don't understand why anyone would want to do this.

The patrons at Benton Lee's Steakhouse are the same folks you see on the church pew Sunday morning, the moms of the elementary school drop-off line and dads of the community ball field. They're Southern folks that do life together, that appreciate a good slab of beef when they see it. This is not an audience

concerned about locally sourced ingredients, a five-star plate presentation, house-made sauces or compound butters. They're not seeking white tablecloths or organic produce, just a place they can go with the family in tow for a hearty meal and a break from cooking themselves. Down home, friendly and no nonsense. My kind of place!

Celebrity guests have included country music sensation Travis Tritt, the late actress Donna Douglas (a.k.a Ellie May Clampett from The Beverly Hillbillies TV Show), Troy and Jacob Landry from the History Channel's Swamp People and Duck Dynasty's Si Robertson. It doesn't get more country than that, folks!

The walls contain an eclectic mix of taxidermy and farm equipment familiar to the South Georgia region. An antique hand mixer and some old Coca-Cola bottles decorated the shelf above our table. Every booth and table in the restaurant houses everything you need – paper towels, salt & pepper, ketchup, steak sauces and hot sauce. A well-lit jukebox stands near the doorway. Attentive servers wear bright pink t-shirts displaying the "Don't Tread on Me" Gadsden Flag.

A sign posted on the front porch of the property sums up the philosophy of Benton Lee's well. It reads:

NOTICE:
This Restaurant is Politically Incorrect
We Say
Merry Christmas
God Bless America
We Salute Our Flag
Give Thanks to Our Troops and We Respect Our Law Enforcement
If this offends you, PLEASE LEAVE
In God We Trust

Come hungry and come as you are.

National TV

My Taste of Hollywood

January 12, 2014

Six days. Five airports. 4,830 miles roundtrip. 35 people from all over the nation.

Over the summer of 2013, I auditioned for Season 2 of ABC's *The Taste*, a cooking competition reality show. After a two-month process of interviews, loads of paperwork and intense anticipation and waiting, I was selected out of thousands to

be among the Top 35 contestants in the nation to compete on the Audition episode which premiered on Jan. 2, 2014 at 8 p.m. They flew me to Los Angeles, California and put me up in a 24-story hotel in the Hollywood Hills where I had a view of the pool, the palm trees and seven lanes of interstate.

This is my story.

I left rural Georgia with my California-titled iPod playlist including Kelly Clarkson's *Breakaway*, Eminem's *Lose Yourself* and Jay-Z and Alicia Keys' *Empire State of Mind*. From the airport, I posted LeAnn Rimes' *One-Way Ticket* music video on Facebook and sang the "Westbound train" lyrics in my head. I was filled with big dreams, confidence and high hopes.

Fast forward through Day 1: I traveled through four time zones, experienced plane delays, checked in at the hotel and got somewhat acquainted. Day 2: I shopped for ingredients. Day 3: On scene at Universal Studios, I was treated like a movie star in a hair & make-up trailer and had my outfit approved by two British people in the wardrobe trailer. On-camera interviews were completed. Day 4: Showtime.

The first 15 minutes of the season on set were mine. I was the first contestant to face the mentors. I'll never forget the moment I entered the set through the "pantry," and rounded the corner to step on stage. There were big lights, lots of extras and over 15 cameras–from every angle–ALL pointed at me. That made some contestants nervous, but I reveled in it. "This is it," I thought. It was my moment to shine. Everything I'd waited for. I gave it to them. I smiled. I played my Southern character with pride, relishing in the fact that I was the only contestant there from Georgia. I lived every moment. As I walked on set, I heard one producer shout to a cameraman, "We got a good one!"

Aside from the challenges I faced, like my first time cooking on a gas stove, using pots and pans I'd never used before, along with shopping in a region where ingredients where titled "Southern Style Grits," I kept a level head and remained cognizant of the time. I was given an hour to cook and plate my signature dish: Shrimp and Grits with a Creamy White Wine Sauce. While chopping vegetables and talking with producers, I burned my first pan of bacon. I also almost mistook lemon grass for my garnish because I couldn't find green onion in the refrigerator. Nevertheless, I kept going.

I finished the challenge with five minutes remaining, having successfully plated my dish and all six tasting portions–two for beauty shots, four for tasting. I put forth the best creamy white wine sauce I'd ever made. Some memories fade and some feelings are fleeting–but one that will remain with me forever is stepping off the set and feeling that rush of fulfillment wash over me. I had done what I came to do, and I had done it well.

Then I exited the stage and was escorted to the friends and family room where I would see my boyfriend, Kurt, and two of my very best friends, Chad and Charity. They were flown out for a three-day period during my stay. Following a brief touch-up with the make-up artist, I opened the door to the family room and saw the people I love sitting on the edge of their seats with expressions of expectation so vivid. We had been separated since the previous day, and the emotion and excitement I expressed was nothing short of real.

After that high, I faced my fate. I would wait for the producer's cue, then walk forward and stand on the spoon-shaped "x marks the spot." There, right in front of my face, just steps away, sat Anthony Bourdain, Nigella Lawson, Marcus Samuelsson and Ludo Lefebvre---in the flesh. It was one of those moments where you're present, but beside yourself. I saw their lips moving and heard them speaking, but had it not been recorded, I would

question if it ever really happened. There I was, a food blogger from small town Blythe, Georgia and Twiggs County farm country, in Hollywood on a set at Universal Studios, in front of these well accomplished, renowned culinary experts. They had just tasted *my* food.

British home cook, food writer and bestselling cookbook author Nigella Lawson was the first to tell me what she thought. Nigella's team is the one I had hoped to join. Nigella and I were wearing the same color–both royal blue dresses, so right off the bat, it was meant to be.

She asked me to introduce myself and tell her a little bit about my dish. She was interested in "the powdered seasoning" I'd used and the spice in the dish. Unfortunately, she'd decided that my shrimp were "slightly overcooked," and the Old Bay seasoning I'd used was too much. "As you know we made our decisions before we met you," she said and with what seemed regretful, she pushed her red "No" button.

I was crushed, and I knew my chances of joining the others' teams were dim. Sure enough, with every comment followed the dreaded red button.

After everything I'd heard about Anthony Bourdain, I must say, I thought he'd be the toughest judge. As it turns out, he was one of the kindest to me. We agreed that food was such a personal thing. "Unfortunately for you, I didn't have an emotional connection to your shrimp and grits," he said. He had been surprised that I wasn't professionally trained though, noting that the Old Bay gave my dish a restaurant quality. That was HUGE coming from a man who's traveled the world. I'll take it.

Marcus Samuelsson said my passion was evident, and that he liked how my dish represented the region of the country from which I came. With a quick and succinct comment, Ludo Lefebvre said "It wasn't my thing. I didn't like it. It's a no."

Everyone has their taste buds, and America would be a boring place if we all liked the same things.

So, as show business would have it, all four of the judges rejected me. It was time to pack it up and head on back to the Peach State, but not before I drank a Shirley Temple on Hollywood Boulevard, got my picture taken in front of the noto-rious HOLLYWOOD sign and took pictures of the stars on the Hollywood Walk of Fame. I exited the hotel with my 50-pound suitcase in tow, containing clothes with the tags still on them, as Adele's *Chasing Pavement* played over the elevator like the well-timed beat of a bass drum.

I won't forget the talented people I got to compete with and the connections I made. I will carry this experience to the grave.

My appreciation for the South has never been greater than when I travel outside the South. I came home with new eyes. At the grocery store in my hometown, as I pushed my buggy through the produce department where I'm known by name, where hardly anything is gluten-free, organic or vegan, and where Johnny Cash plays on the radio, I was home. Home in my Southern, two-lane, suburban, football-loving town. If ever I needed a reminder of exactly who I am, traveling serves its purpose.

One word of advice: No matter the outcome, go after it. Always go after the things that make your heart beat. To quote the one and only Julia Child, "Find something you're passionate about and keep tremendously interested in it."

Dr. Oz's Nationwide Healthy Recipe Challenge

January 24, 2014

Just a few weeks after I was on ABC's *The Taste*, I received an email one evening from producers of The Dr. Oz Show. They had found my blog online and reached out to ask me to represent my home State of Georgia in Dr. Oz's Nationwide Healthy Recipe Challenge. I was asked to submit a healthy version of peach cobbler. Finalists were tasked with creating multiple video clips showcasing how to make their revised recipe at home. Three finalists were chosen to appear on the show to have Dr. Oz taste their dish, with the award being a chance to be featured on Dr. Oz's website for one year as a recipe columnist! Though I wasn't chosen as one of the top three finalists, the video I submitted aired on the show. It was a fun experience, but one I didn't accomplish alone.

I'm a big believer in taking opportunities as they come, but the funny thing is, you don't get to press the pause button on your life to make them happen. This opportunity came with a quick deadline, in the middle of one of my best friend's grandmother's memorial services. I lived in Statesboro, Ga. at the time, and was making the 5-hour trip to Centre, Ala. for the funeral to support my dear friend Chad, who was also singing during the service. I packed up my Grand Prix, my best Bundt cake in tow, and arrived for the visitation, followed by the service and the funeral procession to the cemetery. We celebrated the life of Chad's sweet Amma at the home of his parents with fried chicken and all the fixings, surrounded by family and friends.

Chad Steed and Rebekah

Later that evening, after the emotional toll of the day had taken its course, Chad and I were sitting in his living room, hanging out and taking it easy. By this time, it was nearly midnight, and I was leaving the following day. I had not breathed a word about The Dr. Oz Show, but knew Chad would be the one to help me execute the videos with finesse, and if I was going to do it, now was the time. Chad and I have known each other for years - we met as missionaries in the Golden Isles of Georgia in college - and have a certain level of comfortability with each other that comes from years of rich experiences. I was hesitant to ask him to help because of the sensitivity of my visit, but there was a small part of me that thought, maybe he'd like a distraction. So, I broached the subject, prefacing it with, "You do not have to do this and if you say no, I will completely understand. No hard feelings." He sat up, eyes wide and said, "What?!" I could no longer contain my excitement, and jumped up, gave him the spill and in true genuine friendship without skipping a beat, he matched my excitement jumping up and down, screaming "Oh my gosh, let's do this!" We set about cleaning and staging his kitchen, made a quick run to the grocery store for ingredients and got camera ready.

We had so much fun filming the takes and laughing at ourselves. In one of the clips, Chad had to taste the dish and describe the flavors. After taking a bite, he couldn't seem to describe the dish without repeating the phrase "spot on." He'd say, "Mmm, this is so good, Rebekah. This is spot on." Then at another point while holding my Grilled Georgia Peaches with Toasted Granola and Honey during a final take, a peach fell out of the bowl and hit the counter with a loud thunk! That clip made for a fantastic blooper reel. Chad and I both ended up on the show by video appearance, and though we were only featured for a few quick seconds on TV, we made a lifetime of memories in the process.

Chad, I am forever grateful to you for being willing to entertain my adventures. You never deny me! Thanks for being such a great friend. You'll always be "spot on" in my book.

Grilled Georgia Peaches with Toasted Granola and Local Honey

Serves 2

Ingredients

- 2 Large Georgia Peaches, peeled and cut in half, or 1 bag of frozen, sliced peaches
- ½ – 1 cup of granola, toasted
- Kosher Salt
- 1-2 tbsps of local Tupelo Honey
- Low-fat Vanilla Yogurt or Fat Free Ice Cream
- Butter or Light Non-Stick Cooking Spray

If you've never tasted grilled peaches, start living. When fruit is grilled, the sugars caramelize, making the flavor that much more concentrated and Some Kinda Good. Georgia peaches really shine in this lightened up dessert. While we all know there's no real substitute for one of Georgia's best Southern recipes–good ol' peach cobbler, this dish satisfies your sweet tooth without packing on the pounds. When fresh peaches aren't in season, you can substitute frozen ones. The peaches may also be grilled outside or on an indoor grill pan. Not an ice cream fan? Forgo it and serve it with fresh, sweetened whipped cream instead. My Grilled Georgia peaches with Toasted Granola and Local Honey are fantastic served over pound cake or homemade ice cream.

To grill a fresh peach, slice it right down the middle, remove the pit, brush the halves with melted butter and season with kosher salt. Allow the peach to grill skin side up for about 3-4 minutes. Meanwhile, toast granola in a saucepan over medium heat, about five minutes, stirring slightly, until golden brown and fragrant. Place 1-2 scoops of cold ice cream in a bowl. Top with grilled peaches. Sprinkle with granola and drizzle with honey.

Food Network Here I Come

April 19, 2018

One fine day in the early spring of 2013, I was cruising around Statesboro, Georgia in my black Grand Prix, when I had a light-bulb moment. At the time, I had been blogging for about two years, and as I considered where I wanted to take my food writing and culinary entertainment side gig, I thought, "Some days, all I need is a camera crew." It was a simple idea; one that would soon come to fruition and catapult me into a world of cooking like I had never known before.

Later that summer, I got my camera crew. I became the host and co-producer of Statesboro Cooks, a 30-minute cooking show we filmed right in my tiny kitchen on North Edgewood Drive. That little show was one step in the path I had already begun carving for myself on this crazy, food-loving adventure. Today, in that same spirit of drive and determination, I'm so excited to finally share this announcement: I'M A FINALIST ON SEASON 14 OF FOOD NETWORK STAR! That's right...you'll see ME on the Food Network THIS SUMMER! I'll be competing for the ultimate prize, to host my very own cooking show.

I literally cannot wait to share this journey with you. I've watched this show for so many years from my own couch with my notepad and pen in hand. I always said I would be on it someday, and that day is here folks. Food Network Star dream...check!

Mark your calendars now for the Season Premier on June 10 at 9 p.m. Thank you for all your support as I live out my dreams right before your eyes. Follow *Some Kinda Good* and join me on social media throughout the season where I'll be answering your burning questions and having a ball watching the show, right along with you.

A wise man once told me, you must make your own luck. He was so right. I've never believed in luck, but rather preparation meeting opportunity. There are no secrets to success. It is the result of hard work, learning from failure and being willing to risk it all! I have taken so many steps to prepare for this moment in my life and I truly believe they have all been for such a time as this.

So, here we go, y'all! Cheer me on and wish me good vibes. This Georgia girl is LA bound...bright lights, big city baby!

*You can watch clips from the show on my food blog. Visit SomeKindaGood.com to follow along on my Food Network Star journey. *

Photo Credit: Smallz & Raskind/FoodNetwork.com

Photo Credit: Michael Mariatis/FoodNetwork.com

Photo Credit: Michael Moriatis/FoodNetwork.com

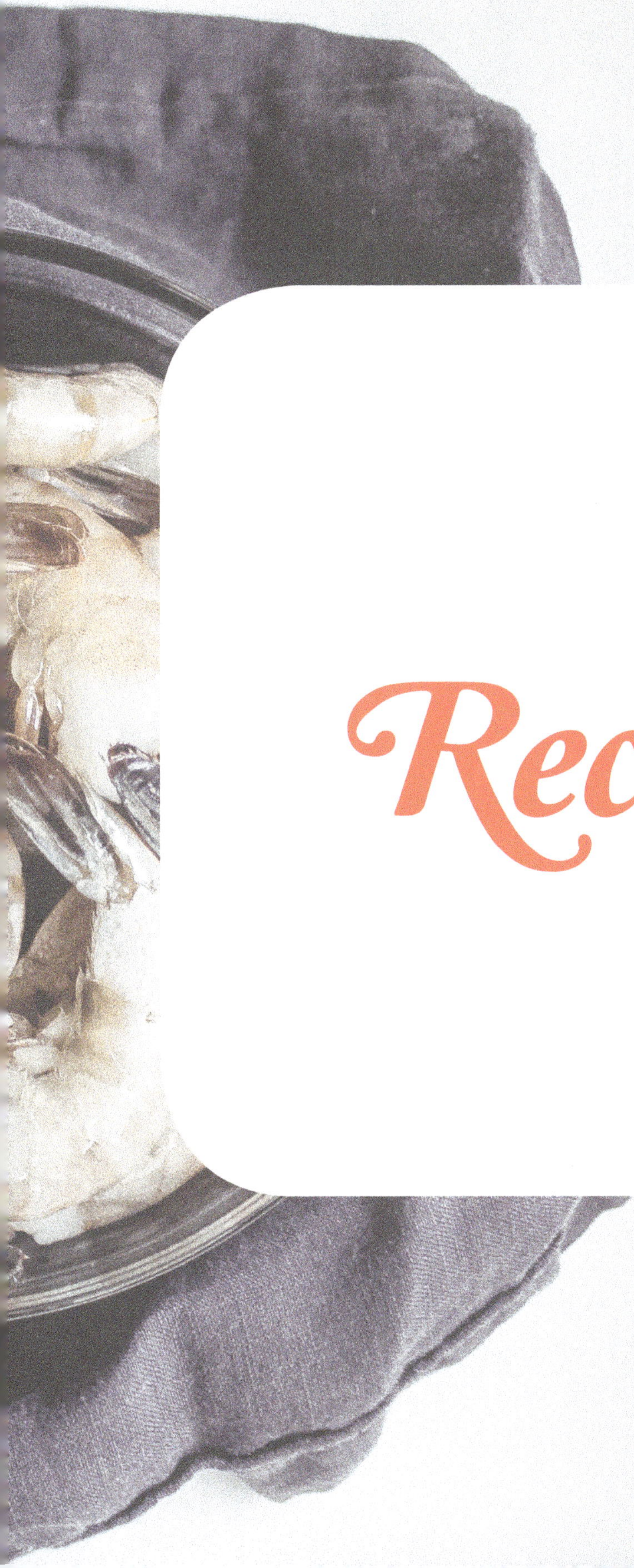

Recipes

Farmers' Market Summer Bruschetta

This Bruschetta was developed in preparation for my live cooking demonstrations at the Statesboro Main Street Farmers' Market. There are never any leftovers. It's perfect for serving as a first course or appetizer with cocktails and makes delicious use of summer's vine-ripened tomatoes and fresh basil.

Serves 4-6

Ingredients

- 2 tbsps of extra virgin olive oil
- 6 cloves of garlic, minced
- Half of 1 medium Vidalia onion, finely chopped
- 2 pints red and yellow grape tomatoes, halved lengthwise
- Balsamic vinegar to taste
- 1 tsp sugar
- 1 bunch fresh basil, separated into leaves, rolled up tightly and sliced (chiffonade)
- Kosher salt and freshly ground black pepper
- 1 Italian baguette
- 1 whole garlic clove, peeled
- 1 stick of butter

Heat olive oil in a medium skillet. Add garlic and onion and stir for about one minute. Pour into a mixing bowl and let cool slightly. Add tomatoes, a splash of balsamic vinegar, sugar and basil. Season to taste with salt & pepper. Toss to coat. If time permits, refrigerate for one hour. If not, it is fine to use immediately. Cut the baguette into diagonal slices. Melt half of the butter in the same skillet you used for the garlic. Toast the baguette on both sides until golden brown. Rub toast with one whole garlic clove while hot. Repeat with remaining butter and bread. To serve, stir the tomato mixture and spoon generously over toasted baguette slices.

Fried Green Tomatoes

SERVES 4-6

INGREDIENTS

- 2 large green tomatoes
- 1 cup all-purpose flour
- 1 tbsp of Old Bay Seasoning
- 1 tbsp of Garlic Powder
- 1 cup plain panko bread crumbs
- 1 egg, beaten
- 2 tbsps water or milk
- Kosher salt and freshly ground black pepper to taste
- Vegetable oil for frying
- Red pepper jelly
- Crumbled goat cheese
- Fresh basil, chiffonade, for garnish

These fried green tomatoes are a hit with my family and friends. The creamy crumbled goat cheese compliments the crispy fried coating and goes great with the kick from the red pepper jelly.

Slice tomatoes about ¼ of an inch thick. Place them in a colander and season with salt. Allow them to drain in the sink for at least 30 minutes. Meanwhile, fill a cast iron skillet or 10-inch frying pan with vegetable oil halfway full and set over medium heat. The oil will be ready for frying when sizzling occurs after gently sprinkled with water. Set up a dredging station: In a small dish, use a fork to combine the flour, Old Bay, salt and pepper. In another small dish, combine the beaten egg with water or milk. In another small dish, combine the Panko bread crumbs with garlic powder. Dredge the tomatoes in the flour mixture, ensuring both sides and edges are evenly coated. Then dredge in the egg wash, followed by the bread crumbs. Shake off any excess before dropping the tomato slices into the hot oil. Fry the tomato slices until golden brown, turning once during cooking. Remove them from the oil and drain on paper towels. Place about 1 tablespoon of red pepper jelly on a serving plate and spread. Top with three fried green tomatoes per serving. Garnish with crumbled goat cheese and fresh basil.

Spicy Pimento Cheese

Serves 8 - 10

Ingredients

- 2 jalapeno peppers, seeded and diced
- ½ Vidalia onion, diced
- 2 cloves fresh garlic, minced
- 2 (4 oz) jars of diced pimento peppers, drained
- ½ (8 oz) block of pepper jack cheese, grated
- ½ (8 oz) block of sharp cheddar cheese, grated
- ½ (8 oz) block of cream cheese, softened
- 2 tbsps of Duke's mayonnaise
- Salt, pepper and Old Bay seasoning to taste

Growing up, I never liked to eat pimento cheese. That was, until I made it myself. In this recipe, I cut back on mayonnaise and use cream cheese instead. This pimento cheese is great on a sandwich, as a dip or melted on toast (under the broiler).

In a medium bowl, blend all ingredients together with a hand mixer. Season well. Serve with crackers and celery for dipping, between two pieces of white bread for a classic Southern sandwich or as a *Some Kinda Good* hamburger topping.

Bacon, Lettuce and Fried Green Tomato (BLFGT) Sliders

I served these sliders at "Nibble & Nosh and Everything Posh," a signature food and style event created by my friend Chad and me, first held in Centre, Alabama. They are one of my favorite ways to eat a fried green tomato.

To assemble a slider, spread pimento cheese onto a Hawaiian Dinner Roll. Top with spring mix lettuce, one fried green tomato and crispy bacon.

resh Alaskan Salmon Cakes with Mango Salsa

Ingredients

For the Salmon Cakes:

- 4 tbsps extra virgin olive oil
- 1lb fresh Salmon, skin removed and finely chopped
- 1 cup Panko bread crumbs
- 4 tbsps sour cream
- Salt and pepper to taste

For the Mango Salsa:

- 1 mango, diced
- 1 tomato, diced
- ¼ cup purple onion, diced
- 1 jalapeno, seeded and diced
- Zest of 1 lime
- Juice of ½ lime
- 1 bunch cilantro, minced
- 1 tsp sugar
- Salt and pepper to taste

Our good friend, Rory, works on a charter boat and marina in Alaska during the summer months. He always returns home with fresh caught salmon and shares it with us. Salmon Cakes are a nice alternative to crab cakes and are a lot less finicky to make. The mango salsa adds a pop of color and a bright, citrusy flavor to the crispy cakes. Serve them as an appetizer or a lovely lunch over greens.

In a cast iron skillet (or standard frying pan), heat olive oil over medium-high heat. Get it good and hot because you want to achieve that nice sear on the salmon cakes. Meanwhile, in a medium bowl, toss together salmon, bread crumbs, sour cream and seasonings. Make 9 (2 1/2 inch) patties. Pan sear them for about 3 minutes on each side. Drain on paper towels and set aside.

In another medium bowl, toss all ingredients together. Garnish with fresh cilantro. Top salmon cakes with salsa.

Aunt Adela's Cold Georgia Blue Crab Dip

In early springtime when the Masters Golf Tournament comes to Augusta, my best friends and I, along with our families escape to St. Simons Island for a week of vacation. Crabbing off the pier is one of the activities we look forward to most, because there's nothing quite as exciting and fun as reeling in your net to find two or three beautiful wild Georgia blue crabs, fresh from the Atlantic Ocean, clinging to your basket. On the first spring break we vacationed together, we caught nine male blue crabs–just enough to make this delectable dip. Angela, my best friend of more than 25 years, taught us how to clean the crabs and pick the meat, and we developed this recipe together. Angela is married to Levi, who spent his summers crabbing in the tidal rivers of Shellman Bluff, while visiting his beloved Aunt Adela. In honor of Aunt Adela, this Cold Georgia Blue Crab Dip is slightly sweet, creamy and has just enough punch from the hot sauce to make you want more.

In a medium bowl, combine the first 11 ingredients until well blended. Gently fold in the crab meat, stirring to combine. Finish the dip with a few dashes of Old Bay right over the top. Chill in the refrigerator for at least 30 minutes or until cold. Serve with buttery crackers. Refrigerate leftovers.

Wild Georgia Shrimp and Grits

This is the recipe I made for celebrity judges on ABC's The Taste. I love cooking it to entertain, especially when wild Georgia shrimp is abundant on the East coast.

Cook grits according to package directions, using chicken broth in place of water. Season with salt and pepper, then add butter and stir in Parmesan cheese. Meanwhile, cook bacon until crisp. Drain on paper towels and set aside. In the bacon fat, sauté the shallot, bell pepper, jalapeno and celery. Cook for 3 – 5 minutes, until vegetables become fragrant and translucent. Add garlic and stir for about 30 seconds. Once vegetables have married together, add the white wine and bring to a boil. Let cook for 2-3 minutes, reducing the liquid slightly. Stir in milk and bring to a boil. Reduce heat to medium-low and simmer for 5 minutes to let the sauce thicken. Season with salt and pepper to taste.

Season shrimp with Old Bay. Add shrimp to sauce and stir. Increase heat to medium, and cook shrimp until they turn pink, about 3 – 4 minutes. Remove from heat. Be careful not to overcook the shrimp.

To plate, heap grits onto a plate and top with shrimp and sauce mixture. Garnish with crumbled bacon, green onion and freshly grated Parmesan cheese.

Wild Georgia Shrimp and Corn Chowder

Ingredients

- 3 slices of hardwood smoked bacon
- 2 stalks celery, thinly sliced
- 2 stems of green onion, chopped, plus more for garnish
- ½ medium Vidalia onion, chopped
- 2 large russet potatoes, peeled and diced
- 3 ears of fresh, summer corn, sliced off the cob
- 3 sprigs lemon thyme
- 2 bay leaves
- Kosher salt and freshly ground pepper
- 2 tbsps all-purpose flour
- 1 quart 2% milk
- 1 lb medium shrimp, peeled and deveined
- Old Bay, for seasoning shrimp

This recipe is best in the summertime when sweet corn on the cob and wild Georgia shrimp are in season, but good quality frozen ingredients will satisfy a craving on cold winter days. The crunch of sweet corn with salty bacon and starchy potatoes come together in complete harmony with wild Georgia shrimp.

In a large skillet with a high rim, cook bacon on medium-high heat. Remove the bacon. In the remaining bacon fat, sauté the celery, green onions and Vidalia onions, potatoes and corn. Add the thyme, bay leaves, 1/2 teaspoon salt and a few grinds of pepper, and cook, stirring, 3 – 5 minutes. Stir in the flour until incorporated, about 2 minutes. Stir in the milk, then cover and bring to a boil. Uncover, reduce the heat to medium-low and gently simmer until the vegetables are tender, about 6 minutes. Discard the thyme sprigs and bay leaves.

Season the shrimp with Old Bay. Stir in the shrimp and cook until opaque, about 4 minutes. Season with salt. Divide among bowls and sprinkle with green onion and chopped bacon. Serve with Italian bread.

Lobster Mac & Cheese

My Lobster Mac & Cheese is creamy with succulent pieces of lump lobster tail in every single bite. Medium-size pasta shells with little ridges are used so the cheese sauce coats the noodles well. Gruyere and sharp cheddar combined with a touch of nutmeg really brings out the nuttiness in the cheeses.

In a large saucepan, make a roux by melting butter and adding flour, whisking to combine. Cook and stir until flour has dissolved and turns light brown in color. In a medium saucepan, heat milk, then add to the roux. Meanwhile, cook pasta according to package directions and set aside. Add grated cheeses to the roux, until the cheese has melted. Add the salt, pepper, cayenne and nutmeg. Remove the cheese sauce from the heat and stir in pasta and lobster meat. Once everything is combined, pour the mixture in a greased 2-quart casserole dish and top with breadcrumbs. Dot the top with butter and bake at 425 for 25 minutes or until the top is golden brown. Garnish with parsley. Let stand 5 minutes before serving.

Jambalaya

Ingredients

- 4 thick slices of bacon, cut into 1 inch pieces
- 1 lb sausage, such as kielbasa or Italian, sliced diagonally
- 2 bell peppers, 1 red and 1 green, diced
- 2 celery ribs, sliced
- 1 large onion, chopped
- 1 jalapeno, seeded and diced
- 2 cloves of garlic, minced
- 2 tbsps of Old Bay
- 1 tbsp Herbs de Provence, crushed
- Salt and pepper to taste
- 1 bay leaf
- 2 tbsps of tomato paste
- 2 cups long grain white rice
- 1 (28 oz) can fire-roasted tomatoes
- 3 cups chicken stock
- 1½ pounds of medium shrimp, peeled and deveined

As a finalist on Food Network Star, this is the first dish I cooked on the show. I will never forget standing in front of Bobby Flay and Giada De Laurentiis as they took a bite. Bobby said, "I love the acidity from the tomatoes and green onion. It has great flavor." Giada said, "The dish is fantastic!" If only I could've convinced her to tip it on back.

Preheat the oven to 350 degrees. In a Dutch oven, fry the bacon pieces until brown, remove from the pan to drain on paper towels and set aside. In the rendered bacon fat, sear the sausage cooking on all sides, then scoop them out and set aside. Add the bell and jalapeno peppers, celery, onion and garlic and stir until fragrant and softened, about 5 minutes. Stir in the seasonings, Old Bay, Herbs de Provence, salt and pepper. Add the tomato paste and rice and stir to toast the rice for 2 minutes. Return bacon and sausage to the pot. Add the chicken stock and bay leaf. Cover the pot with a lid and bring the mixture to a boil. Place the pot in the oven and bake for 25 minutes.

Season shrimp with Old Bay. Remove the pot from the oven and tuck the shrimp into the rice mixture. Place the lid back on the pot and return to the oven to bake until the stock has been absorbed and the rice is tender and moist, 20 – 25 minutes. For an unforgettable, Southern coastal affair, serve with it with my Fried Green Tomatoes.

Cod Fish Tacos

I use cod specifically in these tacos because cod fillets are thick and sturdy. They won't fall apart when dredged, and they aren't so tiny that the other ingredients overpower them. I love that the slaw features vinegar, rather than mayo. The vinegar adds great texture to the slaw and keeps the dish light and fresh. My favorite part about the sauce is the lime zest. Citrus zest wakes up just about any sauce and packs a real flavor punch.

Place a large, high-rimmed skillet over medium-high heat and fill it with about an inch of vegetable oil. Set up a dredging station in three separate dishes. In the first dish, mix flour with seasonings. In the second dish, beat egg slightly, then add milk and stir to combine. In the third dish, place the bread crumbs. Dredge the cubed cod in the order of the dredging station, first in the flour mixture, followed by the egg wash and bread crumbs, ensuring that all sides are coated well. Fry until golden brown, flipping every two minutes or so. Drain the fish on a paper towel lined baking sheet. Before serving tacos, heat tortillas in the microwave for 30 seconds.

For the Avocado Sauce

In a food processor, mix all the ingredients until well blended. Refrigerate until ready to use.

For the Slaw

In a large mixing bowl, combine all the ingredients until well incorporated. Serve with tacos.

Acknowledgements

Starting any new endeavor is always a gamble. It takes guts to put yourself out there, to believe in your own abilities and make a go of it all. You need a tribe, a support system, a die-hard group of people in your corner. You need friends and family who cheer you on and build you up, who tell you the truth even if it's hard to hear. I have accomplished much in my thirty something years, but I have not done it alone. I have been blessed with an amazingly talented group of family and friends, a few of which have been with me from the start of *Some Kinda Good*.

Tori Ivey Sprankle is such a friend. A graphic designer by trade, she's been my girl's night out go-to, my pet sitter, my bridesmaid and my #1 brand ambassador. She's the reason I auditioned for my first cooking competition TV show, *The Taste* on ABC, and she led the design of this book. Tori, thank you for all the creative work you've done for me–the recipe cards, social media graphics, flyers, business cards, posters and even my wedding invitations–all without expecting anything in return. You took my brand from a cute idea to a legitimate logo and captured the essence of the Southern, coastal vibe I envisioned. It's been an honor to work with you through the years, especially on this book, and there's no other designer I would entrust with such a meaningful project and my personal brand. I love you and am proud to count you among my closest friends.

Tyson Davis. Where would I be without you? Thank you for entertaining that first email inquiry from me when I was a complete stranger to you, and for giving me a local platform with

Statesboro Cooks. The cooking shows we filmed together with your students in that tiny, yellow kitchen on North Edgewood Drive are some of my best memories. Cruising around Statesboro in my Grand Prix, you, filming from the passenger's seat, as if I was Ina Garten and you were my camera crew. What is life? What fun we had. Thank you for filming and editing my auditions for cooking competitions on national TV, and for cheering me on every time I called. You not only became my go-to camera man, but a true friend. We did it--we went all the way to ABC and Food Network! I have you to thank for so much. Erin go Bragh!

To **Bill Fortenberry**, my mentor and friend, thank you for nurturing my writing, for taking me under your wing in my first career job out-of-college. You taught me the power of storytelling, how to edit and to ask why. You taught me how to paint a picture with my words and took the time to invest your years of experience in me. I'll never forget the first conversation we had in my third job interview. You reviewed my writing samples and said I demonstrated "real journalistic ability." Your advice and guidance have meant the world to me, and I hope to make you proud.

Daniel Cole. We literally grew up together playing Power Rangers, jumping on the trampoline and "swimming" in mud holes. You were my first best friend when my family moved to Blythe and our moms still talk about how we could play for hours. I'm not surprised that you became an attorney at law; you were always smart and able to hold your own. Thank you for being kind enough to review my national TV contracts for culinary competitions, to explain the legalese speak in layman's terms and to provide guidance on the areas I didn't understand. You went above and beyond. Your reassurance and affirmation pushed me forward in a critical moment of decision, and I will not forget your generosity.

There are a group of girls I've known for nearly 25 years: **Angela Smith, Charity Rauls and Jennifer Allen.** We met in middle school and have remained close friends through the years.

They've been my bridesmaids (on more than one occasion!), the keepers of my secrets and my very best friends in this life, who've always been my amen corner. I could write a book on all our experiences together. Thank you for knowing me and still loving me, for being my confidants when things are good *and* when I've fallen flat on my face, and for encouraging my crazy culinary adventures. Thank you for speaking life over me. I admire each of you for different reasons - your strength, tenacity, inner beauty, faith, grace and triumph over tragedy has inspired me in more ways than I can count. I will always love you.

To **Chad Steed**, you are the male version of me. What's not to love? Thank you for making me laugh so hard I cry, for dancing with me when the music stops, being my ride-or-die friend, fashion consultant and fellow dream chaser. I love your talent, the risks you take and your creative, confident, leap-of-faith-outlook on life. Thank you for always listening and spending hours on the phone, just because we can. We are cut from the same cloth and I will never deny you. Thank you for affirming me in times of doubt and dreaming with me when we were just beginning to realize our potential.

Jenni Williams, we met on the mission field in 2004, and have shared experiences in a third world country that most will never have. You are one of the most generous and beautiful souls I know. I can always count on you for Luke Bryan Farm Tour tickets or a Bahamas cruise and a good time, but most importantly for being there when it counts. Thank you for being my roll-the-windows-down-dance-in-the-car girl and for your uplifting, ever-hospitable friendship.

To my **mom** and **Grandma Dot**, thank you for teaching me the joy of cooking and sharing it with others around the family table. Your recipes and the way you love others through food has had a profound impact on me. Some of my greatest memories are in the kitchen with you. Thank you for being an example of strong, beautiful women and for teaching me what it means to create a home. The long line of good cooks in our family continues with you.

To my brother, **Joey,** a relationship like ours is rare. Thanks for listening and understanding, for your wisdom and reliability. I can always count on you! **Dad,** you are like a solid oak tree, strong and steady, deep-rooted and unswayed by the wind. Thank you for being a constant safe place and rock in my life.

To my handsome husband and #1 taste-tester, **Kurt**, you've always believed in me and are my biggest fan. Thank you for your endless patience when you are hungry and I'm photographing all of our food before we eat, for your tireless encouragement when you have worked all day and are standing behind a camera when you'd much rather be in your chair, while I gather my thoughts before going live on Facebook. Thank you for supporting my wildest dreams, and for holding down the house and taking care of our precious puppy, Ewok, in my absence. I love you. To quote Paul Child, "You are the butter to my bread and the breath to my life."

To the **farmers**, thank you for working so hard to provide our communities with good food. To know each of you is to know where our food comes from and the value of that is priceless.

To **Jim Healy** at the *Statesboro Herald*, thank you for giving me a platform every other week in the newspaper to share my story and recipes. To **Angye Morrison** and **Linsay Cheney Rudd,** thank you for designing my column and making it shine, then and now. Your creativity and attention to detail never goes unnoticed.

Finally, I am sincerely grateful for the **folks** who read my food column, follow my blog and support me on social media. Many of you have read my stories for years, and I always enjoy hearing your feedback. Thank you for making my recipes and for stopping me in the grocery store, at the library, in the neighborhood or at the farmers' market to share your family traditions, cooking victories and mishaps. I cherish your encouragement and friendship and look forward to many more food adventures together.

Additional Praise for **Some Kinda Good**

"Where many students come into culinary school to find themselves and figure out their own culinary style, Rebekah came with a clear, defined culinary story, and all the drive to exceed any challenge put before her. Her ability to combine her career in media with her ongoing ventures in food only strengthens her input in the culinary field. I cannot wait to see what she embarks on next!"

—CHEF ALEX LEWIS,
CEC, M.ED.

"Rebekah invites readers to pull up a chair around the table and pass the time together like old friends. She is real and relatable, and her recipes are easy to follow and delicious."

—CASEY STODDARD,
COMMUNICATIONS COORDINATOR

"With her love of cooking and watching others enjoy the fruits of her labor, Rebekah Lingenfelser is the consummate Southern hostess. But she's also a top-notch storyteller, interjecting humor and warmth into all her writing. You'll enjoy reading about her family traditions and celebrations, and you'll be inspired by her story. And along the way, you just might learn a thing or two. By the end of the book, you're sure to say, that was 'Some Kinda Good.'"

—ANGYE MORRISON,
EDITOR, STATESBORO PUBLISHING

Rebekah F. Lingenfelser
Some Kinda Good

About the Author

Rebekah Faulk Lingenfelser is a culinary TV personality, food enthusiast, writer and speaker. A finalist on *Food Network Star* and ABC's *The Taste*, she is the longtime Statesboro Herald food columnist and creative force behind the Southern coastal brand and blog, *Some Kinda Good*. A Georgia Southern University alumna, Rebekah earned her Bachelor of Science degree in public relations (PR). She also attended Savannah Technical College's Culinary Institute of Savannah. An advocate for supporting local, whether restaurants, farmers' markets or small businesses, Rebekah values cooking with local, in-season ingredients. A firm believer that food tastes best at its peak, she takes pride in showcasing Georgia grown food. Rebekah shares cooking and entertaining tips, and easy-to-execute, flavorful recipes to encourage others to gather around the family table and share in the joy of cooking and eating together. Good food and good company, that's what it's all about!

When she's not cooking up a storm, you can find her singing, reading or boating along the intracoastal waterways of Southeast Georgia. Rebekah works full-time as a PR professional. A member of Community Bible Church, she resides in Savannah with her husband Kurt, and gregarious, 10-pound Shih Tzu, Ewok. Connect with *Some Kinda Good* on social media and learn more by visiting *RebekahLingenfelser.com*.

www.ingramcontent.com/pod-product-compliance
Lightning Source LLC
Chambersburg PA
CBHW040315100426
42811CB00012B/1451